ACKNOWLEDGMENT

The editors gratefully acknowledge Mary Kelsey for her help in the writing and production of this book.

CONTENTS

Introduction

Your resume is your first impression on a prospective employer. Though you may be articulate, intelligent, and charming in person, a poor resume may prevent you from ever having the opportunity to demonstrate your interpersonal skills, because a poor resume may prevent you from ever being called for an interview. While few people have ever been hired solely on the basis of their resume, a well-written, well-organized resume can go a long way toward helping you land an interview. Your resume's main purpose is to get you that interview. The rest is up to you and the employer. If you both feel that you are right for the job and the job is right for you, chances are you will be hired.

A resume must catch the reader's attention yet still be easy to read and to the point. Resume styles have changed over the years. Today, brief and focused resumes are preferred. No longer do employers have the patience, or the time, to review several pages of solid type. A resume should be only one page long, if possible, and never more than two pages. Time is a precious commodity in today's business world and the resume that is concise and straightforward will usually be the one that gets noticed.

Let's not make the mistake, though, of assuming that writing a brief resume means that you can take less care in preparing it. A successful resume takes time and thought, and if you are willing to make the effort, the rewards are well worth it. Think of your resume as a sales tool with the product being you. You want to sell yourself to a prospective employer. This book is designed to help you prepare a resume that will help you further your career—to land that next job, or first job, or to return to the work force after years of absence. So, read on. Make the effort and reap the rewards that a strong resume can bring to your career. Let's get to it!

Chapter One

THE ELEMENTS OF A GOOD RESUME

A winning resume is made of the elements that employers are most interested in seeing when reviewing a job applicant. These basic elements are the essential ingredients of a successful resume and become the actual sections of your resume. The following is a list of elements that may be used in a resume. Some are essential; some are optional. We will be discussing these in this chapter in order to give you a better understanding of each element's role in the makeup of your resume:

1. Heading
2. Objective
3. Work Experience
4. Education
5. Honors
6. Activities
7. Certificates and Licenses
8. Professional Memberships
9. Special Skills
10. Personal Information
11. References

The first step in preparing your resume is to gather together information about yourself and your past accomplishments. Later you will refine this information, rewrite it in the most effective language, and organize it into the most attractive layout. First, let's take a look at each of these important elements individually.

Heading

The heading may seem to be a simple enough element in your resume, but be careful not to take it lightly. The heading should be placed at the top of your resume and should include your name, home address, and telephone numbers. If you can take calls at your current place of business, include your business number, since most employers will attempt to contact you during the business day. If this is not possible, or if you can afford it, purchase an answering machine that allows you to retrieve your messages while you are away from home. This way you can make sure you don't miss important phone calls. *Always* include your phone number on your resume. It is crucial that when prospective employers need to have immediate contact with you, they can.

Objective

When seeking a particular career path, it is important to list a job objective on your resume. This statement helps employers know the direction that you see yourself heading, so that they can determine whether your goals are in line with the position available. The objective is normally one sentence long and describes your employment goals clearly and concisely. See the sample resumes in this book for examples of objective statements.

The job objective will vary depending on the type of person you are, the field you are in, and the type of goals you have. It can be either specific or general, but it should always be to the point.

In some cases, this element is not necessary, but usually it is a good idea to include your objective. It gives your possible future employer an idea of '
want to go.

The objective st.
uncertain of the exa(
inclusion of an overl
your not being cons
you should be sure t
letter, instead.

Work Experience

This element is arguably the most important of them all. It will provide the central focus of your resume, so it is necessary that this section be as complete as possible. Only by examining your work experience in depth can you get to the heart of your accomplishments and present them in a way that demonstrates the strength of your qualifications. Of course, someone just out of school will have less work experience than someone who has been working for a number of years, but the amount of information isn't the most important thing—rather, how it is presented and how it highlights you as a person and as a worker will be what counts.

As you work on this section of your resume, be aware of the need for accuracy. You'll want to include all necessary information about each of your jobs, including job title, dates, employer, city, state, responsibilities, special projects, and accomplishments. Be sure to only list company accomplishments for which you were directly responsible. If you haven't participated in any special projects, that's all right—this area may not be relevant to certain jobs.

The most common way to list your work experience is in *reverse chronological order*. In other words, start with your most recent job and work your way backwards. This way your prospective employer sees your current (and often most important) job before seeing your past jobs. Your most recent position, if the most important, should also be the one that includes the most information, as compared to your previous positions. If you are just out of school, show your summer employment and part-time work, though in this case your education will most likely be more important than your work experience.

The following worksheets will help you gather information about your past jobs.

WORK EXPERIENCE
Job One:

Job Title _____

Dates _____

Employer _____

City, State _____

Major Duties _____

_____

_____

_____

_____

_____

_____

Special Projects _____

_____

_____

_____

Accomplishments _____

_____

_____

Job Two:

Job Title _____

Dates _____

Employer _____

City, State _____

Major Duties _____

_____

_____

_____

_____

_____

_____

Special Projects _____

_____

_____

_____

Accomplishments _____

_____

_____

_____

_____

_____

_____

_____

MER 2011-08-12 12:36
You were helped by mercirc

Job Three:

Job Title _____

Dates _____

Employer _____

City, State _____

Major Duties _____

_____

_____

_____

_____

_____

_____

Special Projects _____

_____

_____

_____

Accomplishments _____

_____

_____

_____

_____

_____

_____

_____

Job Four:

Job Title _____

Dates _____

Employer _____

City, State _____

Major Duties _____

_____

_____

_____

_____

_____

_____

Special Projects _____

_____

_____

Accomplishments _____

_____

_____

_____

_____

_____

_____

_____

Education

Education is the second most important element of a resume. Your educational background is often a deciding factor in an employer's decision to hire you. Be sure to stress your accomplishments in school with the same finesse that you stressed your accomplishments at work. If you are looking for your first job, your education will be your greatest asset, since your work experience will most likely be minimal. In this case, the education section becomes the most important. You will want to be sure to include any degrees or certificates you received, your major area of concentration, any honors, and any relevant activities. Again, be sure to list your most recent schooling first. If you have completed graduate-level work, begin with that and work in reverse chronological order through your undergraduate education. If you have completed an undergraduate degree, you may choose whether to list your high school experience or not. This should be done only if your high school grade-point average was well above average.

The following worksheets will help you gather information for this section of your resume. Also included are supplemental worksheets for honors and for activities. Sometimes honors and activities are listed in a section separate from education, most often near the end of the resume.

EDUCATION

School _____

Major or Area of Concentration _____

Degree _____

Date _____

School _____

Major or Area of Concentration _____

Degree _____

Date _____

Honors

Here, you should list any awards, honors, or memberships in honorary societies that you have received. Usually these are of an academic nature, but they can also be for special achievement in sports, clubs, or other school activities. Always be sure to include the name of the organization honoring you and the date(s) received. Use the worksheet below to help gather your honors information.

HONORS

Honor: _____

Awarding Organization: _____

Date(s): _____

Honor: _____

Awarding Organization: _____

Date(s): _____

Honor: _____

Awarding Organization: _____

Date(s): _____

Honor: _____

Awarding Organization: _____

Date(s): _____

Activities

You may have been active in different organizations or clubs during your years at school; often an employer will look at such involvement as evidence of initiative and dedication. Your ability to take an active role, and even a leadership role, in a group should be included on your resume. Use the worksheet provided to list your activities and accomplishments in this area. In general, you should exclude any organization the name of which indicates the race, creed, sex, age, marital status, color, or nation of origin of its members.

ACTIVITIES

Organization/Activity: _____

Accomplishments: _____

_____

_____

Organization/Activity: _____

Accomplishments: _____

_____

_____

Organization/Activity: _____

Accomplishments: _____

_____

_____

Organization/Activity: _____

Accomplishments: _____

_____

_____

As your work experience increases through the years, your school activities and honors will play less of a role in your resume, and eventually you will most likely only list your degree and any major honors you received. This is due to the fact that, as time goes by, your job performance becomes the most important element in your resume. Through time, your resume should change to reflect this.

Certificates and Licenses

The next potential element of your resume is certificates and licenses. You should list these if the job you are seeking requires them and you, of course, have acquired them. If you have applied for a license, but have not yet received it, use the phrase "application pending."

License requirements vary by state. If you have moved or you are planning to move to another state, be sure to check with the appropriate board or licensing agency in the state in which you are applying for work to be sure that you are aware of all licensing requirements.

Always be sure that all of the information you list is completely accurate. Locate copies of your licenses and certificates and check the exact date and name of the accrediting agency. Use the following worksheet to list your licenses and certificates.

CERTIFICATES AND LICENSES

Name of License: _____

Licensing Agency: _____

Date Issued: _____

Name of License: _____

Licensing Agency: _____

Date Issued: _____

Name of License: _____

Licensing Agency: _____

Date Issued: _____

Professional Memberships

Another potential element in your resume is a section listing professional memberships. Use this section to list involvement in professional associations, unions, and similar organizations. It is to your advantage to list any professional memberships that pertain to the job you are seeking. Be sure to include the dates of your involvement and whether you took part in any special activities or held any offices within the organization. Use the following worksheet to gather your information.

PROFESSIONAL MEMBERSHIPS

Name of Organization: _____

Offices Held: _____

Activities: _____

Date(s): _____

Name of Organization: _____

Offices Held: _____

Activities: _____

Date(s): _____

Name of Organization: _____

Offices Held: _____

Activities: _____

Date(s): _____

Name of Organization: _____

Offices Held: _____

Activities: _____

Date(s): _____

Special Skills

This section of your resume is set aside for mentioning any special abilities you have that could relate to the job you are seeking. This is the part of your resume where you have the opportunity to demonstrate certain talents and experiences that are not necessarily a part of your educational or work experience. Common examples include fluency in a foreign language, or knowledge of a particular computer application.

Special skills can encompass a wide range of your talents—remember to be sure that whatever skills you list relate to the type of work you are looking for.

Personal Information

Some people include "Personal" information on their resumes. This is not generally recommended, but you might wish to include it if you think that something in your personal life, such as a hobby or talent, has some bearing on the position you are seeking. This type of information is often referred to at the beginning of an interview, when it is used as an "ice breaker." Of course, personal information regarding age, marital status, race, religion, or sexual preference should never appear on any resume.

References

References are not usually listed on the resume, but a prospective employer needs to know that you have references who may be contacted if necessary. All that is necessary to include in your resume regarding references is a sentence at the bottom stating, "References are available upon request." If a prospective employer requests a list of references, be sure to have one ready. Also, check with whomever you list to see if it is all right for you to use them as a reference. Forewarn them that they may receive a call regarding a reference for you. This way they can be prepared to give you the best reference possible.

Chapter Two

WRITING YOUR RESUME

*N*ow that you have gathered together all of the information for each of the sections of your resume, it's time to write out each section in a way that will get the attention of whoever is reviewing it. The type of language you use in your resume will affect its success. You want to take the information you have gathered and translate it into a language that will cause a potential employer to sit up and take notice.

Resume writing is not like expository writing or creative writing. It embodies a functional, direct writing style and focuses on the use of action words. By using action words in your writing, you more effectively stress past accomplishments. Action words help demonstrate your initiative and highlight your talents. Always use verbs that show strength and reflect the qualities of a "doer." By using action words, you characterize yourself as a person who takes action, and this will impress potential employers.

The following is a list of verbs commonly used in resume writing. Use this list to choose the action words that can help your resume become a strong one:

administered	introduced
advised	invented
analyzed	maintained
arranged	managed
assembled	met with
assumed responsibility	motivated
billed	negotiated
built	operated
carried out	orchestrated
channeled	ordered
collected	organized
communicated	oversaw
compiled	performed
completed	planned
conducted	prepared
contacted	presented
contracted	produced
coordinated	programmed
counseled	published
created	purchased
cut	recommended
designed	recorded
determined	reduced
developed	referred
directed	represented
dispatched	researched
distributed	reviewed
documented	saved
edited	screened
established	served as
expanded	served on
functioned as	sold
gathered	suggested
handled	supervised
hired	taught
implemented	tested
improved	trained
inspected	typed
interviewed	wrote

Now take a look at the information you put down on the work experience worksheets. Take that information and rewrite it in paragraph form, using verbs to highlight your actions and accomplishments. Let's look at an example, remembering that what matters here is the writing style, and not the particular job responsibilities given in our sample.

WORK EXPERIENCE
Regional Sales Manager

Manager of sales representatives from seven states. Responsible for twelve food chain accounts in the East. In charge of directing the sales force in planned selling toward specific goals. Supervisor and trainer of new sales representatives. Consulting for customers in the areas of inventory management and quality control.

Special Projects: Coordinator and sponsor of annual food industry sales seminar.

Accomplishments: Monthly regional volume went up 25 percent during my tenure while, at the same time, a proper sales/cost ratio was maintained. Customer/company relations improved significantly.

Below is the rewritten version of this information, using action words. Notice how much stronger it sounds.

WORK EXPERIENCE
Regional Sales Manager

Managed sales representatives from seven states. Handled twelve food chain accounts in the eastern United States. Directed the sales force in planned selling towards specific goals. Supervised and trained new sales representatives. Consulted for customers in the areas of inventory management and quality control. Coordinated and sponsored the annual Food Industry Seminar. Increased monthly regional volume 25 percent and helped to improve customer/company relations during my tenure.

Another way of constructing the work experience section is by using actual job descriptions. Job descriptions are rarely written using the proper resume language, but they do include all the information necessary to create this section of your resume. Take the description of one of the jobs your are including on your resume (if you have access to it), and turn it into an action-oriented paragraph. Below is an example of a job description followed by a version of the same description written using action words. Again, pay attention to the style of writing, as the details of your own work experience will be unique.

PUBLIC ADMINISTRATOR I

Responsibilities: Coordinate and direct public services to meet the needs of the nation, state, or community. Analyze problems; work with special committees and public agencies; recommend solutions to governing bodies.

Aptitudes and Skills: Ability to relate to and communicate with people; solve complex problems through analysis; plan, organize, and implement policies and programs. Knowledge of political systems; financial management; personnel administration; program evaluation; organizational theory.

WORK EXPERIENCE
Public Administrator I

Wrote pamphlets and conducted discussion groups to inform citizens of legislative processes and consumer issues. Organized and supervised 25 interviewers. Trained interviewers in effective communication skills.

Now that you have learned how to word your resume, you are ready for the next step in your quest for a winning resume: assembly and layout.

Chapter Three

ASSEMBLY AND LAYOUT

*A*t this point, you've gathered all the necessary information for your resume, and you've rewritten it using the language necessary to impress potential employers. Your next step is to assemble these elements in a logical order and then to lay them out on the page neatly and attractively in order to achieve the desired effect: getting that interview.

Assembly

The order of the elements in a resume makes a difference in its overall effect. Obviously, you would not want to put your name and address in the middle of the resume or your special skills section at the top. You want to put the elements in an order that stresses your most important achievements, not the less pertinent information. For example, if you recently graduated from school and have no full-time work experience, you will want to list your education before you list any part-time jobs you may have held during school. On the other hand, if you have been gainfully employed for several years and currently hold an important position in your company, you will want to list your work experience ahead of your education, which has become less pertinent with time.

There are some elements that are always included in your resume and some that are optional. Following is a list of essential and optional elements:

Essential	*Optional*
Name	Job Objective
Address	Honors
Phone Number	Special Skills
Work Experience	Professional Memberships
Education	Activities
References Phrase	Certificates and Licenses
	Personal Information

Your choice of optional sections depends on your own background and employment needs. Always use information that will put you and your abilities in a favorable light. If your honors are impressive, then be sure to include them in your resume. If your activities in school demonstrate particular talents necessary for the job you are seeking, then allow space for a section on activities. Each resume is unique, just as each person is unique.

Types of Resumes

So far, our discussion about resumes has involved the most common type—the *reverse chronological* resume, in which your most recent job is listed first and so on. This is the type of resume usually preferred by human resources directors, and it is the one most frequently used. However, in some cases this style of presentation is not the most effective way to highlight your skills and accomplishments.

For someone reentering the work force after many years or someone looking to change career fields, the *functional resume* may work best. This type of resume focuses more on achievement and less on the sequence of your work history. In the functional resume, your experience is presented by what you have accomplished and the skills you have developed in your past work.

A functional resume can be assembled from the same information you collected for your chronological resume. The main difference lies in how you organize this information. Essentially, the work experience section becomes two sections, with your job duties and accomplishments comprising one section and your employer's name, city, state, your position, and the dates employed making up another section. The first section is placed near the top of the resume, just below the job objective section, and can be called *Accomplishments* or *Achievements*. The second section, containing the bare essentials of your employment history, should come after the accomplishments section and can be titled *Work Experience* or *Employment History*. The other sections of your resume remain the same. The work experience section is the only one affected in the functional resume. By placing the section that focuses on your achievements first, you thereby draw attention to these achievements. This puts less emphasis on who you worked for and more emphasis on what you did and what you are capable of doing.

For someone changing careers, emphasis on skills and achievements is essential. The identities of previous employers, which may be unrelated to one's new job field, need to be downplayed. The functional resume accomplishes this task. For someone reentering the work force after many years, a functional resume is the obvious choice. If you lack full-time work experience, you will need to draw attention away from this fact and instead focus on your skills and abilities gained possibly through volunteer activities or part-time work. Education may also play a more important role in this resume.

Which type of resume is right for you will depend on your own personal circumstances. It may be helpful to create a chronological *and* a functional resume and then compare the two to find out which is more suitable. The sample resumes found in this book include both chronological and functional resumes. Use these resumes as guides to help you decide on the content and appearance of your own resume.

Layout

Once you have decided which elements to include in your resume and you have arranged them in an order that makes sense and emphasizes your achievements and abilities, then it is time to work on the physical layout of your resume.

There is no single appropriate layout that applies to every resume, but there are a few basic rules to follow in putting your resume on paper:

1. Leave a comfortable margin on the sides, top, and bottom of the page (usually 1 to 1½ inches).

2. Use appropriate spacing between the sections (usually 2 to 3 line spaces are adequate).

3. Be consistent in the *type* of headings you use for the different sections of your resume. For example, if you capitalize the heading EMPLOYMENT HISTORY, don't use initial capitals and underlining for a heading of equal importance, such as Education.

4. Always try to fit your resume onto one page. If you are having trouble fitting all your information onto one page, perhaps you are trying to say too much. Try to edit out any repetitive or unnecessary information or possibly shorten descriptions of earlier jobs. Be ruthless. Maybe you've included too many optional sections.

CHRONOLOGICAL RESUME

LISA P. CHINCHIOLO

237 HAMMAN DRIVE
CHICAGO, IL 60606
(312)555-3368

OBJECTIVE:	A part-time position in a florist shop.
EXPERIENCE:	
1993 - 1994	THE BUD SHOP

- Made bouquets
- Cared for plants and fresh flowers
- Operated a cash register
- Interacted with customers

1990 - 1991   VALLEY RANCH HOMES

- Maintained plants for model homes

1987 - 1990   HOUSE AND LAWN CARE

- Did odd jobs for area houses
- Mowed and watered lawns
- Watched houses and pets
- Did some landscaping and painting

EDUCATION: Hamman High School, Chicago, IL
Expected graduation date: 1994
GPA 4.00/4.00

Plans include attending Harold
Washington College, Chicago, IL.

SCHOOL ACTIVITIES: Member of the Chicago Scholarship
Federation. Attended all meetings and
participated in activities.

Four-year member of the Horticulture
Club. Final year as President.

*ADDITIONAL
INFORMATION:*   I have received only As in school, and
will graduate from Hamman High School as
valedictorian with honors in science.

REFERENCES WILL BE MADE AVAILABLE UPON YOUR REQUEST.

FUNCTIONAL RESUME

BRIAN KANEKO

Permanent Address:
57 Rochester Way
Marietta, GA 30060
(404)555-5445

Present Address:
P.O. Box 4855
Berkeley, CA 94720
(415)555-1007

OBJECTIVE: An entry-level position in construction management utilizing my technical, organizational, and interpersonal skills to assist with project control tasks.

EDUCATION: **University of California/Berkeley**, Berkeley, CA
Department of Civil Engineering
Master of Science Degree Candidate, May 1995
GPA: 3.89/4.00

Harvey Mudd College, Claremont, CA
School of Civil Environmental Engineering
Bachelor of Science Degree, May 1992
GPA: 3.90/4.00

COURSE WORK: Civil Engineering Materials, Construction Project Organization and Control, Risk Analysis and Management, Construction Management, Heavy Construction and Earthwork, Legal Aspects of the Construction Process, Decision Analysis in Construction.

EXPERIENCE: **Research Assistant**   Summer 1994
California Transportation Institution, Stockton, CA. Researched several design and construction-related areas of bituminous materials as part of the Strategic Highway Research Program, sponsored by the Federal Highway Administration.

Staff Engineer   Summers 1992 - 1993
Thompson Engineers, Marietta, GA. Assisted the preparation of a complete operation and maintenance manual for a leachate treatment plant. Provided support in the compilation and review of all operation and maintenance-related submittals from the general contractor and all subcontractors.

ACHIEVEMENTS: Engineer-in-Training (EIT) Certification
Dean's List, University of California/Berkeley
Graduate Assistantship, University of California/Berkeley
Dean's List, Harvey Mudd College

SKILLS: Computer Languages: Fortran, Pascal, Basic, Lotus 1-2-3, SuperCalc, Excel, SAS, AutoCAD. Fluent in Japanese.

REFERENCES: Available upon request.

Don't let the idea of having to tell every detail about your life get in the way of producing a resume that is simple and straightforward. The more compact your resume, the easier it will be to read and the better an impression it will make for you.

In some cases, the resume will not fit on a single page, even after extensive editing. In such cases, the resume should be printed on two pages so as not to compromise clarity or appearance. Each page of a two-page resume should be marked clearly with your name and the page number, e.g., "Judith Ramirez, page 1 of 2." The pages should then be stapled together.

Try experimenting with various layouts until you find one that looks good to you. Always show your final layout to other people and ask them what they like or dislike about it, and what impresses them most about your resume. Make sure that is what you want most to emphasize. If it isn't, you may want to consider making changes in your layout until the necessary information is emphasized. Use the sample resumes in this book to get some ideas for laying out your resume.

Putting Your Resume in Print

Your resume should be typed or printed on good quality $8^{1}/_{2}$″ × 11″ bond paper. You want to make as good an impression as possible with your resume; therefore, quality paper is a necessity. If you have access to a word processor with a good printer, or know of someone who does, make use of it. Typewritten resumes should only be used when there are no other options available.

After you have produced a clean original, you will want to make duplicate copies of it. Usually a copy shop is your best bet for producing copies without smudges or streaks. Make sure you have the copy shop use quality bond paper for all copies of your resume. Ask for a sample copy before they run your entire order. After copies are made, check each copy for cleanliness and clarity.

Another more costly option is to have your resume typeset and printed by a printer. This will provide the most attractive resume of all. If you anticipate needing a lot of copies of your resume, the cost of having it typeset may be justified.

Proofreading

After you have finished typing the master copy of your resume and before you go to have it copied or printed, you must thoroughly check it for typing and spelling errors. Have several people read it over just in case you may have missed an error. Misspelled words and typing mistakes will not make a good impression on a prospective employer, as they are a bad reflection on your writing ability and your attention to detail. With thorough and conscientious proofreading, these mistakes can be avoided.

The following are some rules of capitalization and punctuation that may come in handy when proofreading your resume:

Rules of Capitalization

- Capitalize proper nouns, such as names of schools, colleges, and universities, names of companies, and brand names of products.
- Capitalize major words in the names and titles of books, tests, and articles that appear in the body of your resume.
- Capitalize words in major section headings of your resume.
- Do not capitalize words just because they seem important.
- When in doubt, consult a manual of style such as *Words Into Type* (Prentice-Hall), or *The Chicago Manual of Style* (The University of Chicago Press). Your local library can help you locate these and other reference books.

Rules of Punctuation

- Use a comma to separate words in a series.
- Use a semicolon to separate series of words that already include commas within the series.
- Use a semicolon to separate independent clauses that are not joined by a conjunction.
- Use a period to end a sentence.
- Use a colon to show that the examples or details that follow expand or amplify the preceding phrase.
- Avoid the use of dashes.
- Avoid the use of brackets.
- If you use any punctuation in an unusual way in your resume, be consistent in its use.
- Whenever you are uncertain, consult a style manual.

Chapter Four

THE COVER LETTER

*O*nce your resume has been assembled, laid out, and printed to your satisfaction, the next and final step before distribution is to write your cover letter. Though there may be instances where you deliver your resume in person, most often you will be sending it through the mail. Resumes sent through the mail always need an accompanying letter that briefly introduces you and your resume. The purpose of the cover letter is to get a potential employer to read your resume, just as the purpose of your resume is to get that same potential employer to call you for an interview.

Like your resume, your cover letter should be clean, neat, and direct. A cover letter usually includes the following information:

1. Your name and address.

2. The date.

3. The name and address of the person and company to whom you are sending your resume.

4. The salutation ("Dear Mr." or "Dear Ms." followed by the person's last name, or "To Whom It May Concern").

5. An opening paragraph explaining why you are writing (in response to an ad, the result of a previous meeting, at the suggestion of someone you both know) and indicating your interest in the job being offered.

6. One or two more paragraphs that tell why you want to work for the company and what qualifications and experience you can bring to that company.

7. A final paragraph that closes the letter and requests that you be contacted for an interview. You may mention here that your references are available upon request.

8. The closing ("Sincerely," or "Yours Truly," followed by your signature with your name typed under it).

Your cover letter, including all of the information above, should be no more than one page in length. The language used should be polite, businesslike, and to the point. Do not attempt to tell your life story in the cover letter. A long and cluttered letter will only serve to put off the reader. Remember, you only need to mention a few of your accomplishments and skills in the cover letter. The rest of your information is in your resume. Each and every achievement should not be mentioned twice. If your cover letter is a success, your resume will be read and all pertinent information reviewed by your prospective employer.

Producing the Cover Letter

Cover letters should always be typed individually, since they are always written to particular individuals and companies. Never use a form letter for your cover letter. Each one should be as personal as possible. Of course, once you have written and rewritten your first cover letter to the point where you are satisfied with it, you certainly can use similar wording in subsequent letters.

After you have typed your cover letter on quality bond paper, be sure to proofread it as thoroughly as you did your resume. Again, spelling errors are a sure sign of carelessness, and you don't want that to be a part of your first impression on a prospective employer. Make sure to handle the letter and resume carefully to avoid any smudges, and then mail both your cover letter and resume in an appropriate sized envelope. Be sure to keep an accurate record of all the resumes you send out and the results of each mailing.

Numerous sample cover letters appear at the end of the book. Use them as models for your own cover letter or to get an idea of how cover letters are put together. Remember, every one is unique and depends on the particular circumstances of the individual writing it and the job for which he or she is applying.

About a week after mailing resumes and cover letters to potential employers, you will want to contact them by telephone. Confirm that your resume arrived, and ask whether an interview might be possible. Getting your foot in the door during this call is half the battle of a job search, and a strong resume and cover letter will help you immeasurably.

Chapter Five

SAMPLE RESUMES

This chapter contains dozens of sample resumes for people pursuing a wide variety of jobs and careers.

There are many different styles of resumes in terms of graphic layout and presentation of information. These samples also represent people with varying amounts of education and experience. Use these samples to model your own resume after. Choose one resume, or borrow elements from several different resumes to help you construct your own.

Timothy J. Comer

3825 West Thunderbird Way
Three Lakes, WI 54562
(715)555-1878

Objective: Summer employment in which I can work and serve people. Salaried position preferred.

Education: Three Lakes High School, 1990-1994
General education/honor and advanced placement courses.

Experience:

1991-1993 <u>Snowy Sam's Restaurant</u>, Eagle River, WI. Sales and Cleaning. Responsibilities included: opening, preparing all food, dealing with customers, keeping track of money, balancing the money at the end of the day, and securing the building.

Capabilities:
- Excellent organizational skills
- Responsible
- Proficient in the use of cash registers and Macintosh computers
- Ability to work well with people
- Skilled in working independently

Achievements:

1993-1994
- Commissioner of Homecoming and Elections, Associated Student Body; Principal's Honor Roll

1992-1993
- Class Treasurer; Principal's Honor Roll

1991-1992
- Commissioner of Desegregation, Associated Student Body; Principal's Honor Roll

1990-1991
- Principal's Honor Roll

Affiliations:
- Three Lakes Football Team
- Three Lakes Track and Field Team
- Three Lakes Associated Student Body

Awards:
- Three Lakes Football Scout Team Player of the Year, 1993
- Outstanding Leadership Award, Class of 1994

References: Available upon request

MICHAEL SUTHERLAND

2757 Dolphin Dr. • Arnold, MD 21012 • (301)555-5390

Education	**UCLA School of Theater, Film, and TV**, Fall 1994 to present

- Comprehensive Major: Directing and Theater Management

Arnold High School, September 1990 to June 1994
- Forensics Competitive Speech Team (4 yrs.)
- Drama and Musical Productions (3 yrs.)

Awards
- Bank of Maryland Fine Arts Award - 2nd place Region Finals Scholarship, 1994
- Veterans of Foreign Wars Speech Award, 1993 and 1994
- Student of the Year - Arnold High School, 1993
- State Forensics for Thematic Interpretation - 21st place (Pieces included: Torch Song Trilogy, Into the Woods, Brighton Beach Memoirs, and Measure for Measure), 1993
- Rotary Speech Award, 1991 and 1992
- Walter Johnson Musical Comedy Award at Anne Arundel Community Stage, 1991

Performance Theater Experience

- Director, Collaborator, and Performer AIDS Teen Theater, 1994
- "Billy Crocker" in Anything Goes, 1993
- "Vincentio" in Taming of the Shrew, 1993
- "Albert" in Bye Bye Birdie, 1992
- "Frank Butler" in Annie Get Your Gun, 1991
- "Charlie" in Charlie and the Chocolate Factory, 1991
- "Ed" in You Can't Take it With You, 1991
- Writer and Performer AIDS Teen Theater, 1990 and 1991

Technical and Managing Theater Experience

Anne Arundel Community Stage
- Production Assistant - Fiddler on the Roof, 1993
- Assistant Stage Manager - Into the Woods, 1992
- Assistant Stage Manager - Camelot, 1991
- Chorus and Stage Hand - Evita, 1990
- Stage Hand - My Fair Lady, 1991

Peace Child
- Assistant Stage Manager, Props Assistant, 1990
- Assistant Technical Director, USA/USSR Production, 1990

References   Available upon request

Jennifer Rosales
381 Ponderosa Avenue
Albuquerque, NM 87198
(505)555-3578

Work Experience

August 18, 1993 to May 22, 1994
Food Service Worker. KFC, Albuquerque, NM.
Responsibilities: taking and preparing food orders, operating cash register, stocking supplies, and cleaning kitchen and eating areas.

May 10, 1993 to August 1, 1993
Receptionist. Santa Fe Real Estate Company, Albuquerque, NM.
Responsibilities: answering phones and calling customers for further information pertaining to their homes.

Prior to May 1993
Baby-sitter.

Other Experience

★ I am a student in O.W.E., "Outside Work Experience," learning about jobs and future careers.
★ I am fluent in Spanish.
★ I was a camp counselor working with children aged 11-13, assisting with sports and recreational activities.
★ I was a member of the following Albuquerque High School clubs: Unity Among Us, Student Body Council, and "Going Places Academically."

Education

★ I am a graduate of Albuquerque High School, 1994.
★ My grade point average was 2.85/4.00.
★ My educational plans are to attend National College.

References

Available upon request.

JONATHAN DEAN COURIER
8638 Walter Drive
Evanston, IL 60204
(708)555-4825

CAREER OBJECTIVE

An engineering position involving civil/structural analysis and design.

EDUCATION

Northwestern University
Master of Science degree in Civil Engineering
Credits completed towards degree: 21/33

Bachelor of Science degree in Civil Engineering, 1992
Major: Structural Engineering
Minors: Geotechnical Engineering and Construction

Engineer in Training, Illinois

WORK EXPERIENCE

Summer 1993   **Elijah's Architects & Engineers, Inc., Chicago, IL**
Engineering Intern
Worked in the structural division, dealing with the design of criminal justice and educational facilities.

1992-1993   **School of Civil Engineering, Northwestern University**
Teaching Assistant
Helped with Architectural Engineering, Structural Steel Design, and Senior Design classes. Instructed students and graded student work.

Summer 1992   **Engineering Buildings, Northwestern University**
Building Receiving Technician
Handled various assignments during the final construction phases of new additions to campus buildings.

ACTIVITIES AND HONORS

Distinguished Student, Fall 1991
Student Member, American Society of Civil Engineers (ASCE)
Theta Chi Honorary: Marshal, Spring 1991 and President, Fall 1991

REFERENCES AVAILABLE UPON REQUEST

ANTHONY GONZALES

Campus Address:
434 J Pierce Hall
Arizona State University
Tempe, AZ 85287
(602)555-1328

Permanent Address:
836 High Street
Reno, NV 89512
(702)555-7206

OBJECTIVE: To obtain a position as an engineer in the field of civil engineering.

EDUCATION: Arizona State University - 1994
BS Civil Engineering with a structural engineering emphasis.

EXPERIENCE: PRIORITY COURIER, Reno, NV.
Courier
- Picked up and delivered bank bags.
- Handled special delivery of packages and letters for customers.
Summer 1993

YOUTH CONSERVATION CORPS, Reno, NV.
Maintenance Worker
- Involved with upkeep and improvement of state park trails.
- Constructed fence to protect state park nature preserve.
Summer 1992

CHARLIE'S BAR AND GRILL, Reno, NV.
Bus Boy
- Cleared tables.
- Replenished supplies as needed.
Summer 1987 through June 1991

ACTIVITIES: Member, National Eagle Scout Association.
Member, American Society of Civil Engineers.

REFERENCES: Available upon request.

JOSEPHINE ELIZABETH CROCKER

P.O. Box 317 A
Trenton, NJ 08625
(609)555-4832

OBJECTIVE: To gain an entry-level position in the environmental field with a firm offering advanced training.

EDUCATION AND TRAINING

- BS Environmental Health Science, Trenton State College, Trenton, NJ. 1990-1994. 3.2 GPA in major, 2.8 GPA overall.

COURSES
Principles and Practices of Environmental Health
Accident and Disaster Control
Technical Seminar in Environmental Health
Public Health Administration
Microbiology
Epidemiology
Health Biostatistics
Public Health Education
Administrative Seminar
Practicum in Environmental Health
Organic Chemistry
Applied Microbiology

- Internship, Oneida County Health Department, Environmental Division. May-August 1992.
- Internship, Vilas County Health Department, Environmental Division. May-August 1991.

AWARDS AND HONORS

- Inter-sorority Council Outstanding Greek Woman, 1992.
- *Who's Who Among Students in American Universities and Colleges*, 1992.
- Order of Chi Omega Greek Honorary, 1992.
- Inter-sorority Council Most Outstanding Spring President, 1991.
- Inter-sorority Council Most Outstanding Chapter Member, 1991.
- Society of Distinguished Collegiate Americans, 1990.

ACTIVITIES

- Chi Omega, President.
- Inter-sorority Council, Chief Justice of Judicial Board.
- UCP Telethon, Phone Bank Coordinator.

REFERENCES: Will be provided on request.

CINDY MILLER
6652 E. Laurel Road
Cleveland, OH 44106
(216)555-4331

CAREER OBJECTIVE
To secure a position emphasizing engineering and managerial skills with a firm engaged in building construction operations.

EDUCATION
Rutgers - The State University of New Jersey: College of Engineering
New Brunswick, NJ
> Bachelor of Science, May 1994 GPA: 4.6/6.0
> Major: Construction Engineering and Management

Significant Courses:
- Construction Estimating
- Construction Scheduling
- Computer Programming
- Construction Management
- Labor Relations
- Finance and Accounting
- Technical Graphics
- Surveying

Curriculum focused on group projects: Developed complete schematic design and preliminary construction plans for a real facility.

EMPLOYMENT EXPERIENCE
Granite Construction Company, Watsonville, CA
Field Engineer/Scheduler Summer 1993 60 Hours/Week
> Responsibilities:
- project layout
- project checkout
- scheduling of job activities
- organizational preparation

Granite Construction Company, Birmingham, AL
Estimator Summer 1992 48 Hours/Week
> Responsibilities:
- document distribution
- quantity takeoffs from prints
- data entry
- conceptual takeoffs from sketches

Granite Construction Company, Fort Worth, TX
Field Engineer/Tracker Summer 1991 40 Hours/Week
> Responsibilities:
- project layout
- project checkout
- tracking job progression
- laborer

ACTIVITIES
- Associated Builders and Contractors Advertising Committee
- Intramural team sports: volleyball and badminton
- Volunteer fund-raiser for university phone-a-thon

REFERENCES AVAILABLE UPON REQUEST

BARBARA M. SWEENEY

Permanent: 256 Dove Lane
Tampa, FL 33614
(813)555-6901

Current: P.O. Box 1259
Evanston, IL 60204
(708)555-3246

EDUCATION:

Northwestern University, Evanston, IL.
Bachelor of Arts degree in Public Policy Studies, May 1994.
Course Work: Macroeconomics; Microeconomics; Economic Analysis for Public Policy Making; Leadership and Policy Change; Policy Analysis for Public Policy Making; Managerial Effectiveness; Policy Choice and Value Conflict; Analytical Methods for Public Policy Making; Statistical Quantitative Political Analysis.

Sorbonne, Paris, France.
Course Work: French language, art, and history.
Sorbonne College Faculty Honors List, Fall 1993.

WORK EXPERIENCE:

Council for Entrepreneurial Development, Durham, NC.
Management Intern. Oversaw weekly "Entrepreneur's Page" in *Triangle Business Journal*. Contacted area business leaders to match article topics with knowledgeable authors. Edited and compiled all contributions as well as personally wrote additional pieces. *Summer 1993.*

Triangle Business Journal, Raleigh, NC.
Advertising and Promotion Intern. Created advertisements, took photographs for ads, sold advertising space, promoted the *Triangle Business Journal*, and prospected for new advertisers. *Summer 1992.*

First National Bank, Durham, NC.
Cost-Cutting Analyst. Analyzed existing personal computer allocation and purchasing. Proposed, developed, and instituted cost-cutting measures for existing systems. Implemented technology purchasing procedures. Worked in Consumer Services Group, County Corporate Office. *Summer 1991.*

OUTSIDE INTERESTS:
- Northwestern Club Soccer - Treasurer - 1993.
- Wayne Manor Selective House - Selection Committee and Social Chairman - 1993.
- GALS Little League Softball Coach - 1990-1992.
- Intramural Sports - soccer, basketball, flag football.

REFERENCES:
Available upon request.

GEORGE WILLIAM COX

502 Sleigh Street   223 Lindsay Lane
Stockton, CA 95211   Baltimore, MD 21217
(209)555-2416   (301)555-2913

EDUCATION

University of the Pacific, Stockton, CA
B.A. Political Science
GPA: 3.3 on 4.0 scale   Dean's List, 1992-1993
Course Work: Financial Accounting, Policy Analysis Methods,
                     Statistical Analysis, Managerial Effectiveness,
                     Economics, Calculus, Management, and Labor Relations.

Summer in Berlin Program, University of the Pacific
Studied German Reformation, Art History.

FINANCIAL EXPERIENCE

International Swap Dealers Association, New York, NY
Summer Associate, Summer 1993
Reported directly to executive director and senior staff at 200-member
international trade association. Conducted extensive research on
emerging markets and new derivative products. Planned and organized
international swap conference. Produced historical data trend analysis
based on past interest rate and currency swap data.

University of the Pacific Auxiliary Finance Office, Stockton, CA
Senior Accounting Clerk, Summer 1992
Reconciled accounts receivable and payable. Collected past due
balances. Researched and responded to vendor inquiries.

Prudential-Bache Securities, Boston, MA
Investment Broker Assistant, Summer 1991
Gained strong foundation in fundamental principles and practices of
investment decision-making. Helped broker analyze and interpret data
relating to his clients' accounts.

OTHER EXPERIENCE

University of the Pacific Biology-Forestry Library, Stockton, CA
Library Assistant, Academic years 1991-1993
Responsible for operation of circulation desk and reserve collections as
part of work-study program.

USA TODAY, Arlington, VA
Mail Clerk, Summer 1990
Sorted and delivered large volumes of incoming mail. Expedited the
requests of top editors and management including rush deliveries and
special-handling packages.

INTERESTS

Camping, Fishing, Basketball, Coaching.

SKILLS

WordPerfect, Microsoft Word, and MacWrite word processing programs.

REFERENCES
Available upon request.

BRIAN KANEKO

Permanent Address:
57 Rochester Way
Marietta, GA 30060
(404)555-5445

Present Address:
P.O. Box 4855
Berkeley, CA 94720
(415)555-1007

OBJECTIVE: An entry-level position in construction management utilizing my technical, organizational, and interpersonal skills to assist with project control tasks.

EDUCATION: **University of California/Berkeley**, Berkeley, CA
Department of Civil Engineering
Master of Science Degree Candidate, May 1995
GPA: 3.89/4.00

Harvey Mudd College, Claremont, CA
School of Civil Environmental Engineering
Bachelor of Science Degree, May 1992
GPA: 3.90/4.00

COURSE WORK: Civil Engineering Materials, Construction Project Organization and Control, Risk Analysis and Management, Construction Management, Heavy Construction and Earthwork, Legal Aspects of the Construction Process, Decision Analysis in Construction.

EXPERIENCE: **Research Assistant** Summer 1994
California Transportation Institution, Stockton, CA. Researched several design and construction-related areas of bituminous materials as part of the Strategic Highway Research Program, sponsored by the Federal Highway Administration.

Staff Engineer Summers 1992 - 1993
Thompson Engineers, Marietta, GA. Assisted the preparation of a complete operation and maintenance manual for a leachate treatment plant. Provided support in the compilation and review of all operation and maintenance-related submittals from the general contractor and all subcontractors.

ACHIEVEMENTS: Engineer-in-Training (EIT) Certification
Dean's List, University of California/Berkeley
Graduate Assistantship, University of California/Berkeley
Dean's List, Harvey Mudd College

SKILLS: Computer Languages: Fortran, Pascal, Basic, Lotus 1-2-3, SuperCalc, Excel, SAS, AutoCAD. Fluent in Japanese.

REFERENCES: Available upon request.

NAME: Jane Palmer

ADDRESS: 4838 Mercy Street
Carmel, IN 46032
(317)555-2831

OBJECTIVE: To obtain employment as an accountant.

EDUCATION: Kalamazoo College, Kalamazoo, MI, 1994
BA, Economics and Business Administration
GPA 3.75/4.00

COURSE WORK: Economics, managerial accounting, computer science, calculus, linear algebra, and multivariable calculus.

EXPERIENCE:

6/93 - 7/93   **Assistant to Public Relations Director**, United States National Hard Courts, Indianapolis, IN. Typed press releases, updated drawsheets, filed tournament and player data, and answered phones.

5/93 - 6/93   **Tennis Instructor**, Clay Jr. High School, Carmel, IN. Evaluated players, developed lesson plans, and gave group instruction to children and adults.

6/92 - 8/92   **Tennis Camp Instructor and Counselor**, Kalamazoo College, Kalamazoo, MI. Instructed and supervised junior players, organized personal help sessions, and evaluated students.

6/91 - 9/91   **Medical Transcriber**, Dr. Sam Perkins, Family Physician, Carmel, IN. Updated patients' files with information involving diagnosis and treatment and answered phone calls.

ADDITIONAL INFORMATION:

- Member, Alpha Lambda Delta, a college freshman national honorary society.
- Freshman member of the National Collegiate Athletic Association Division III runner-up varsity tennis team at Kalamazoo College.
- All-State high school varsity tennis team.
- Elected to *Who's Who in American High Schools*.
- Read, write, and speak German.

REFERENCES: Will be provided upon request.

BEVERLY M. LEBLANC
P.O. Box 8175
Creighton University
Omaha, NE 68178
(402)555-3686

OBJECTIVE
Environmental engineer position involved with the design of wastewater/water treatment systems, groundwater quality, remediation, groundwater modeling, and hazardous wastes site investigation.

EDUCATION
<u>Creighton University</u> - Omaha, NE
Master of Science in Engineering - 1994
Major: Environmental Engineering
Overall GPA: 3.64/4.00 Major GPA: 3.84/4.00

<u>University of Minnesota</u> - Minneapolis, MN
Bachelor of Science Engineering - 1991
Major: Mechanical Engineering
Overall GPA: 3.55/4.00 Major GPA: 3.75/4.00

TECHNICAL SKILLS

- <u>Major Advanced Courses</u>:
  Water Quality Analysis, Water Treatment Plant Design, Land Treatment of Wastes, Wastewater Treatment Plant Design, Industrial Wastes Treatment, and Sanitary Engineering.

- <u>Computer Languages</u>:   Basic, Fortran
- <u>Operating Systems</u>:   MS DOS/OS2,OS/MVS
- <u>Hardware</u>:   IBM 3278, PDP 11/70, IBM PC/AT/XT
- <u>Software</u>:   WordPerfect, SAS, dBaseIII, Grapher

EXPERIENCE

Fall 1992-present <u>Graduate Research Assistant</u>
Environmental Engineering Department
Creighton University

Monitoring the operating and treatment efficiency of Rotating Biological Contractors.

Summer 1991 <u>Programmer</u>
Environmental Engineering Department
University of Minnesota

Summer 1990 <u>Operator</u>
Minneapolis-St. Paul Wastewater Treatment Plant
Minneapolis, MN

Monitored routine operation of facility.

Summer 1989 <u>Laboratory Analyst</u>
Science Department
University of Minnesota

ACTIVITIES
- Member of Civil Engineering Honor Society
- Student member of ASCE, WPCF, NSPE

REFERENCES
Will be provided on request

KELLY JOHNSON
1546 Balstrode Way
Des Moines, IA 50312
(515)555-2376

OBJECTIVE: To obtain a position working in either a restaurant or drug store.

EDUCATION: St. John's High School, 1994
GPA 4.00/4.00
My educational plans are to attend a four-year state college.

COURSE WORK: Calculus, Typing, Introduction to Business, and Spanish.

AFFILIATIONS: Girl's High School Swim Team
Interact - A community service club
Area Representative - Senior
Vice President - Junior
Community Commissioner - Sophomore
Secretary - Freshman

WORK EXPERIENCE:

6/93-8/93   Round Table Pizza. Cook and Waitress. Assembling pizzas, serving customers and taking their orders, answering phones, and cleaning the restaurant.

6/92-8/92   Prairie Landscapes. Receptionist. Responsible for answering phones and typing memos.

Weekends   Baby-sitting.

OTHER EXPERIENCE: Studied Spanish for five years.

OUTSIDE INTERESTS: Reading, playing the piano, and swimming.

REFERENCES: Available upon request.

HEATHER MORENO

48 Hickory Drive
Houston, TX 77002
(713)555-4968

OBJECTIVE: To obtain a position in the secretarial field.

EDUCATION: Victoria High School, 1994
GPA 3.80/4.00
My educational plans include attending a four-year college.

COURSE WORK: Typing
Accounting
Mathematics
Computer Literacy
Psychology

ACTIVITIES:
- Council Member of Victoria High School Student Government
- Lead Dancer of Flamenco Dance Group
- Candy Striper at Memorial Hospital

WORK EXPERIENCE:

6/93 - 12/93   **Patterson Prizes, Inc.,** *Receptionist.* Answered the phone, entered names into a computer, cleaned, and lifted boxes.

INTERESTS: Jogging
Dancing
Reading
Cooking

REFERENCES: Available upon request

ANTHONY J. RUELAS

364 Sidewinder Way
Lubbock, TX 79409
(806)555-0923

POSITION DESIRED: Political Aide

EDUCATION: Lubbock High School, 1994
GPA 3.70/4.00
I plan to attend Rice University.

COURSE WORK: Political Science I,II
World History
Computer Literacy
Advanced Speech

ACTIVITIES: Associated Student Body President
Student Council, Representative
Special Education Community
   Advisory Committee

WORK EXPERIENCE: **OFFICE ASSISTANT**, Summer 1993
Network Real Estate

PAGE, September 1992 - February 1993
U.S. House of Representatives

REFERENCES: Upon request

KRISTEN GONZALES

11998 Freedom Blvd.
Seattle, WA 98122
(206)555-4691

**POSITION
DESIRED:**   A salaried community service position
enabling me to work with and help others.

EDUCATION: Seattle High School, 1994
GPA 3.50/4.00, four-year member of honor
society.

I plan to attend the University of Washington
in order to obtain a degree in psychology.

**SCHOLASTIC
ACTIVITIES:**   Sophomore Class President
Associated Student Body Member
Commissioner of Hospitality
Soccer Team Member
Softball Team Member

**OUTSIDE
INTERESTS:**   Writing
Soccer
Softball
Reading
Swimming

SKILLS: Speak fluent Spanish
Type thirty words per minute

**WORK
EXPERIENCE:**   **Walmart**, Seattle, WA
Merchandise Cashier
5-92 to 9-94

REFERENCES: Available upon request.

NATHAN MOYA
5620 York Ave. South
Beaverton, OR 97005
(503)555-4159

GOAL: To display my diligent work ethic while gaining solid work experience.

EDUCATION: Beaverton High School, 1994
GPA 3.50/4.00
I plan to attend Oregon State University and continue my education at Law School.

COURSE WORK: Leadership class - organization, leadership, responsibility
Geometry - abstract thinking
Composition - writing structure and clarity

ACTIVITIES: Student Trustee to the School Board
Swim Team
Track and Field Team
Member - Associated Student Body
Boy Scouts - Life Rank
Volunteer - AIDS Quilt, 1993
Volunteer - Food Bank, 1992

INTERESTS: Swimming
Backpacking
Running
Hiking
Cycling

SKILLS: Fluent in Spanish
Computer literate - Macintosh and IBM

WORK EXPERIENCE: Taco Bell Summer 1994 Serve customers.

Ed's Upholstery 1992-1993 Picked up and delivered furniture, cleaned shop.

REFERENCES: Available on request

Marybeth A. Whittle

5679 Opal Cliff
Edmonds, WA 98020
(206)555-2177

GOAL To obtain a position in which I can demonstrate my ability to handle challenging tasks.

EDUCATION Edmonds High School, 1994
GPA 3.80/4.00
Next fall I will attend Georgetown University. After completing my college education, I plan to enter law school.

SCHOOL ACTIVITIES Cheerleading
Associated Student Body - Secretary
Site Council Member
Key Club - community service club member

WORK EXPERIENCE
Summer 1993 Jennifer's Bakery - operated cash register, cleaned.

INTERESTS Running
Knitting

PERSONAL I am a responsible individual who enjoys working with others.

REFERENCES Available upon request.

ELIZABETH M. LEIGH-WOOD

387 SUNNY HILLS DRIVE
MADISON, WI 53711
(608)555-1524

OBJECTIVE	A position as a lifeguard. I am certified in Standard First Aid and CPR and have passed a lifeguard training course.
EDUCATION	▪ <u>Madison High School</u>, 1994 GPA 3.80/4.00 General Education/Honor Classes ▪ Next year I will attend University of Wisconsin in Madison on a swimming scholarship.
SCHOOL ACTIVITIES	▪ Four-year Member of Associated Student Body Council ▪ Four-year Member of Wisconsin Scholarship Federation ▪ Four-year Member of Varsity Swim Team ▪ Two-year Member of Varsity Track Team
ACTIVITIES	▪ 1993-1994: Hospital Volunteer ▪ 1992-1994: American Cancer Society Volunteer Christmas Gift Wrapper
SKILLS	▪ Fluent in French ▪ Hardworking and outgoing
WORK EXPERIENCE	▪ Whalers' Car Wash, 5/93-10/93 ▪ Lifeguard, 5/92-8/92 ▪ Baby-sitting, weekends
REFERENCES	Upon request

SERENA STRELITZ

6450 DORIS AVENUE
SALT LAKE CITY, UT 84112
(801)555-0211

OBJECTIVE: I am seeking a job in sales, either clothing or food.

EDUCATION: Salt Lake City High School, 1994
GPA 4.25/4.00
General Education/Honor and Advanced
Placement Classes

I will attend Brigham Young University in Provo, UT next academic year. I plan to obtain a bachelor's degree in communication.

SKILLS:
- Fluent in German
- Hardworking
- Congenial worker

WORK EXPERIENCE: Worked in the <u>Farm Bakery</u> - salesperson.
November 1993 to April 1994.

Worked in the <u>Snack Shack</u> at football games - salesperson, cashier, and cook.
August to October, 1991 to 1993.

SCHOOL ACTIVITIES:
- Three-year member of *Interact*, a community service club
- Three-year member of *Key Club,* a community service club
- Four-year member of *Utah Scholarship Federation,* including one year as president
- Two-year member of *Varsity Track Team*

VOLUNTEER WORK:
- I spent one year as an assistant in a first-grade class, 1994.

REFERENCES: Available upon request.

MATTHEW BERDAL
351 Huntington Drive
Jacksonville, FL 32211
(904)555-5050

GOAL: A position using my skills as a specialist in PC software training and network support.

QUALIFICATIONS:
- Expert troubleshooter and problem solver.
- Proven ability to educate and motivate others.
- Proficient in PC software and hardware.

EDUCATION: Jacksonville University, Jacksonville, FL
BS Computer Science, 1993   GPA 3.8/4.0

TRAINING:
- MAI Basic Four - Intermediate Business Basic
- Programming
- DEC - PCSA/VAX Based Server System Management
- DEC - Network Management I
- DEC - VAX/VMS System Management I

EMPLOYMENT HISTORY:

INFO TEC Video Systems, Jacksonville, FL
PC Specialist, 1994 - present
Programmer, 1993

Bob'S Family Market, Jacksonville, FL
Manager, 1990 - 1992

PROFESSIONAL EXPERIENCE:

- Acted as administrator for ALL-IN-1 electronic mail on a VAX 4000, with the integration of PC word processing documents and spreadsheets.
- Provided technical consulting to managers demonstrating comprehensive awareness of staff needs.
- Designed and presented training classes on PC software, DOS, and PC fundamentals.
- Instructed company personnel on an individual basis.
- Trained PC users nationwide via telephone.
- Repaired and upgraded all components of TC hardware: AST, AT&T, Compaq, HP, IBM, and Epson.

REFERENCES: Available upon request.

CARLOS RAMIREZ

529 Venetian Way   Boston, MA 02167   (617)555-6053

OBJECTIVE: To obtain a position in management or finance.

EDUCATION: Harvard Graduate School of Business Administration
Candidate for MBA degree, June 1994
Columbia University, BA Economics, 1989

**PROFESSIONAL
EXPERIENCE:**

Summer 1993   **PITTMAN EQUITIES CORPORATION**, Boston, MA
Investment Processor

Responsible for operation of personal computer systems, design and preparation of company sales reports and financial reports, and design of the company's databases using Personal Decision Series software.

1989 - 1992   **McCORMICK COMPANY**, New York, NY
Manager and Director of Investment Services

Managed all aspects of a 40-node 3Com 3Plus Local Area Network, including software configuration and installation, user maintenance, file maintenance, backup procedures, and all day-to-day operations.   Responsible for portfolio analysis and account management in Investment Services Department.

**MICROCOMPUTER
EXPERIENCE:**
- Programs and Softwares: Wordstar and Microsoft Word, Computer-Aided Design and Drafting, and Statistical Analysis System
- Personal Computers: IBM, Apple, Computer Vision, and Macintosh

INTERESTS: Traveling, water skiing, and reading.

REFERENCES: Available upon request.

Marvin Hopkins

341 Beach Pines Drive   Olympia, WA 98505   (206)555-2397

Objective   To work as a project engineer with a computer manufacturer and advance to a management position in research and development.

Education   Eastern Washington University, Cheney, WA
BS Computer and Information Sciences, 1994.

Technical Summary

Software: Allways, Blast, Cross Talk, DrawPartner, Lotus 1-2-3, Norton Utilities, PopTerm, WordPerfect 5.1, Wordstar 2000+, and XTree Gold.

Hardware: IBM personal computers, Macintosh computers, Laserjet printers, modems, plotters, scanners, and Data General mainframe.

Languages: Pascal, BASIC, Cobol, Fortran, and Dataflex.

Summer Work Experience

1992-1993   Microsoft - Redmond, WA
Assistant Systems Manager - Member of four-person team that installed and implemented a 60-node 3Com 3Plus Local Area Network, including 53 IBM-compatible personal computers and 9 Macintosh computers. Provided support for Electronic Mail, WordPerfect 5.1, and Lotus 1-2-3.

1991   MCCAW Cellular Communications - Kirkland, WA
Programmer and Educator - Provided support for all aspects of IBM-compatible personal computers, including software.

References   Work and education references on request.

Willing to relocate

Sarah Louise Hill

865 Woodside Drive
Chattanooga, TN 37403
(615)555-0469

PROFESSIONAL OBJECTIVE:	To gain a position as a marketing representative with possibility of advancement into a managerial position.
EDUCATION:	UNIVERSITY OF TENNESSEE Chattanooga, TN B.S., Business Administration, anticipated May 1995.

EXPERIENCE:

Summer 1993 & 1994	UNION PLANTERS CORPORATION OF AMERICA Nashville, TN <u>Sales Representative</u>: Responsible for service and sales in the Nashville area. Increased sales by 5% each summer. Awarded the 1994 Murphy's Trophy for achieving sales expectancy in every product line.
Summer 1992	HEALTHTRUST Nashville, TN <u>Sales Representative</u>: Achieved 150% expected quota for June to August calling on business and industrial accounts in Tennessee. Ranked #1 out of 12 salespeople.
Summer 1991	A & P SUPERMARKET Nashville, TN <u>Cashier</u>: Dealt with customers and sackers. Handled shift drawer reconciliation.

HOBBIES AND INTERESTS:	Golf, softball, family activities, travel, volunteer work.
REFERENCES:	References will be provided upon request.

WILLING TO RELOCATE

RACHEL DURRAN

298 Cass Street   P.O. Box 1048
Salem, OR 97309   Eugene, OR 97405
(503)555-5329   (503)555-5917

OBJECTIVE

To serve as a receptionist in the executive suite of a large corporation.

EDUCATION

Lane Community College, Eugene, OR, 1994
Degree - Business and Office Technician

ACHIEVEMENTS

Lane Community College Dean's List, December 1993
Lane Community College "Student of the Month," October 1993
Certificates of Achievement for accounting, English, and spelling
Oregon Girl's State Representative, 1989
Student Body Treasurer, Salem High School, 1989-1990
Who's Who on the West Coast, 1990 ed.

SKILLS

Computer, telex, teletype and telecopier operation
Machine transcription
Typing, 85 wpm

EXPERIENCE

RECEPTIONIST - U.S. BANKCORP, Portland, OR, Summers 1992, 1993.
Job included: typing, filing, and processing mail.

RECEPTIONIST - William H. Schmeida M.D., Salem, OR, Summer 1991.
Job included: handling monthly reports, typing, processing mail, and filing
general correspondence material.

REFERENCES

Available upon request.

NOLAN T. YU

Present Address: P.O. Box 61434
Cambridge, MA 02139
(617)555-6087

Permanent Address: 1534 Elm Street
Catonsville, MD 21228
(301)555-6053

Objective: To obtain a position in finance or consulting that requires technical expertise.

Education: MASSACHUSETTS INSTITUTE OF TECHNOLOGY, Cambridge, MA
BS Computer and Information Sciences
June 1994, GPA: 3.5/4.0

Experience: MIT BOOKSTORE
Loss Prevention Agent
Coordinated shrinkage control system, which included the compilation of monthly reports on loss prediction data and statistics. Division reduced inventory loss due to theft by 12%. (2/94 - 6/94)

MIT DINING SOCIETY
Financial Manager
Coordinated a quarterly budget of $65,000. Investigated and analyzed budgetary problems. Revised financial accounting system and established mechanisms for the analysis of fiscal progress through implementation of a data base management software system. (9/92 - 6/93)

**Additional
Information:** Fluent in Chinese
MIT pre-business society
MIT Engineering Association
Varsity tennis team
Experienced with Macintosh and IBM software

References available upon request.

LORETTA M. ALSTON

305 DORIS AVENUE
BALDWIN CITY, KS 66006
(913)555-0211

OBJECTIVE	I would like a position in which my secretarial skills, ability to organize, and willingness to assume responsibility can be employed.
EDUCATION	Baker University, Baldwin City, KS Major: English Literature

EXPERIENCE

Summers
1993 - 1994

REINHARDT & ASSOCIATES LAW CORPORATION
Baldwin City, KS
Personal Secretary for Michael J. Green

- Composed and prepared correspondence
- Handled accounts receivable
- Performed receptionist and general secretarial duties

Summer
1992

SPEEDO INC.
Baldwin City, KS
Secretary

- Performed data entry on IBM PC AT
- Maintained mailing list database
- Purchased office supplies

Summers
1991 - 1990

EXECUTIVE SUNN CENTERS
Baldwin City, KS
Receptionist

ADDITIONAL
INFORMATION

I am familiar with these computer programs: Lotus 1-2-3, MS-DOS, WordPerfect, PC Write, Print Master, and Apparel Pro.

I can type 72 words per minute.

REFERENCES   Are available upon request.

Charles P. Bhatia

Campus Address: Permanent Address:
P.O. Box 7327   234 Rose Street
Henniker, NH 03242   Greenville, IL 62246
(603)555-7123   (618)555-4335

Objective   To obtain a position in manufacturing, analysis, or project
                       development.

Education   <u>New England College</u>, Henniker, NH.
                       Pursuing BS in Industrial Engineering, June 1995. GPA: 3.5/4.0.
                       Responsible for 20% of college expenses.

Experience
6/94 - 9/94   **Management Engineering Intern**
                       <u>Greenville Health Center</u>, Greenville, IL.
                       Analyzed work flow and made recommendations to hospital
                       administrator. Built computerized daily productivity report and
                       employee database file converters. Led team in continuous process
                       improvement project, which involved extensive interviewing.

1/92 - 6/93   **Student Manager**
                       <u>Bon Appetit</u>, Henniker, NH.
                       Interviewed and trained new and current employees. Scheduled
                       workers and reduced labor costs significantly. Planned strategies with
                       director of retail. Changed and improved products. Inventoried and
                       ordered food products weekly. Served and cashiered.

Activities
8/93 - 5/94   **Student Government Association Member**
                       Henniker, NH.
                       Coordinated survey of 2,000 undergraduate classes as assistant director
                       of course evaluations. Debated proposed legislation as the
                       representative for the undergraduate academic council. Oversaw
                       student election process on the ethics committee.

9/91 - 6/94   **Team/Urban Community Vision/Community Volunteer**
                       Henniker, NH.
                       Tutored underprivileged children weekly at their schools.
                       Programmed children's retreat.

Computer Skills   Computer knowledge includes SAS, WordPerfect, Lotus 1-2-3, Excel,
                       programming in PASCAL.

Interests   Scuba diving, sailing, hiking, photography.

NAME	**VICTORIA ALEXANDER FLYNN**

ADDRESS	4678 Freedom Blvd. Newark, DE 19716	**TELEPHONE** (302)555-4780

CAREER OBJECTIVE

A growth-oriented position in human resources management

EDUCATION

University of Delaware, Newark, DE
Master in Business Administration, 1994

Goldey Beacom College, Wilmington, DE
BS, Business and Management, 1992

SUMMER WORK EXPERIENCE

1993 and 1994

KELSEY TECHNOLOGIES CORPORATION
Member of team whose responsibilities included:
- Contingency plan development/implementation
- Administration of various salaried benefit programs
- Hourly and salaried technical training
- Salary planning

1991 and 1992

NEWARK PUBLIC SCHOOLS
Teacher's aide whose responsibilities included:
- Instruction of Business Law, Business Management, and Accounting to high school juniors and seniors
- Curriculum development

ADDITIONAL INFORMATION

Four varsity letters in field hockey, Wilmington, DE
Three varsity letters in track and field, Wilmington, DE
Assistant coach, Wilmington High School field hockey team

REFERENCES

Available upon request

PHILIP E. GADBAW

1625 SOUTH SYLVESTER STREET	P.O. BOX 9087
CRESTVIEW HILLS, KY 41017	BOWLING GREEN, KY 42101
(606)555-2368	(502)555-9850

OBJECTIVE: A position in product/brand marketing offering exposure to product planning and development, market research, and advertising.

EDUCATION: WESTERN KENTUCKY UNIVERSITY
Master of Business Administration, 1994
GPA 4.00/4.00
A broad graduate program in marketing and finance, supported by course work in management, business planning, operations, economics, and accounting.

GLENVILLE STATE COLLEGE
Bachelor of Science degree in Industrial Engineering, 1990
GPA 3.80/4.00
Extensive course work in economics, math statistics, and communications art.

EXPERIENCE: LIBERTY NATIONAL BANCORP   Louisville, KY
Summers 1992, 1993

Industrial Engineer
Designed, performed, and presented factory and office productivity studies with measured savings in excess of $100,000 per study. Accomplishments included the successful engineering, organizing, and presenting of projects and layouts involving expenditures up to $150,000.

HUMANA   Louisville, KY
Summer 1991

Packaging Engineer
Initiated cost savings for June/August period.

CIRCUIT CITY STORES   Glenville, WV
Summer 1990

Engineering Internship
Responsibilities included routing, structuring of bill of materials, and supervising hourly employees.

REFERENCES: Available upon request.

CRAIG L. HJORRING

31 Anderson Road ● **Fort Collins, CO 80523** ● **(303)555-0469**

OBJECTIVE

Management position with special emphasis in marketing and sales.

EDUCATION

Colorado State University, Fort Collins, CO
B.S. in Business Administration and Management expected May 1994
GPA 3.49/4.00

EXPERIENCE

Sutherland Sports Wear   *Assistant Regional Sales Manager*   Summers, 1991-1993

ACHIEVEMENTS

Orchestrated and created all sales literature and advertising. Decreased advertising costs from 5.0% to 3.2% of sales.

Increased sales more than 14% from June to August each summer.

Acquired industry contacts providing for joint ventures with suppliers and customers as member of sales team.

MEMBERSHIPS

Society of Manufacturing Engineers
Fabricating Manufacturers Association

PERSONAL

I enjoy biking, swimming, and family activities.

REFERENCES

Available upon request.

CHRISTOPHER J. HEALY

142 Peachtree Lane
Montgomery, AL 36195
(205)555-9484

OBJECTIVE   *To obtain a position within a marketing or general management firm.*

EDUCATION   **Alabama State University**, *Montgomery, AL - 1994*
Master's degree in Business Administration and Management

Bachelor's degree in Accounting
GPA 4.00/4.00

HONORS   *Beta Gamma Sigma*
Business/Management Honorary
Accounting Honorary

PART-TIME WORK
EXPERIENCE   **Head Coach for Montgomery Summer Basketball League**. *Organized and directed four winning teams, including Sectional and Cluster Champions. June to August, 1993 and 1994*

Assistant Coach for Montgomery Summer Basketball League. *June to August, 1992 and 1993*

Waiter at Max's Bar and Grill. *Primarily served food, occasionally helped clean and clear the tables. June to August, 1989, 1990, and 1991*

REFERENCES   *Furnished upon request*

NICOLE ANNE CHANG

Address: 3089 Mc Glenn Drive
Jonesboro, AR 72467   (501)555-9268

Objective: Position as a veterinarian's assistant, 30 to 35 hours
per week, preferably with a regular schedule.

Education: Arkansas State University; Jonesboro, AR - 1993
B.S. in Veterinary
GPA - 3.24/4.00

Awards: Member of Dean's List - 1993
All-Academic Soccer Team - 1993
High School All-American Soccer Player - 1989

Experience: *Veterinarian Assistant Volunteer*, Michael Stein's
Veterinary Hospital. June to August, 1992 and 1993

Assisted with the administration of medicine and
pacification of the animals.

Assistant Coach, Jonesboro Summer Soccer
League. June and July, 1990 to 1994

Personal: I am a very patient and caring person.
I love working with animals.
I am willing to relocate.

References on request

CHRISTOPHER M. ISEBRAND

2711 Mar Vista Drive
Farmington, CT 06032
(203)555-8900

OBJECTIVE

A position as a technician or an assembler.

BACKGROUND SUMMARY

Possess analytical, technical, and managerial skills. Communicate effectively with corporate representatives and government inspectors. Ability to think in an objective manner. Have excellent problem-solving skills. Work habits are clean and organized.

EDUCATION

U.S. Navy
Avionics Electronics classes

Central Connecticut State University, New Britain, CT
B.S., Engineering Technology, 1979
Minor - Manufacturing Technology
GPA - 3.56/4.00

Farmington High School, Farmington, CT
Diploma, 1975
General Education

EXPERIENCE

U.S. Navy, Aviation Electrician, 1980 - 1994
Received an honorable discharge

REFERENCES

Available upon request.

MELISSA L. JUNG

1530 HANSEN LANE
DOVER, DE 19901
(302)555-9401

OBJECTIVE: To secure employment as an elementary education teacher.

EDUCATION: University of Delaware, Newark, DE - 1971
M.A., Education

Wesley College, Dover, DE - 1969
B.A., Elementary Education
GPA 3.90/4.00

**VOLUNTEER
EXPERIENCE:** Assistant teacher of the arts, Dover Elementary School.

Five-year member Dover Rotary Club. Head of fundraiser to finance a new local elementary school. Raised $32,000.

Weekly volunteer at local homeless soup kitchen.

Hostess for six exchange students from France, Germany, and Japan.

PERSONAL: Homemaker 1974 - present.

I assist my husband in his business by delivering merchandise, purchasing supplies, and arranging financing.

I enjoy swimming, biking, and traveling.

REFERENCES: Available upon request.

CURTIS WENDLE SIMMONS
6542 Jackson Blvd.
La Mesa, California, 91941
(619)555-3428

EMPLOYMENT OBJECTIVE
A career in aviation beginning as airplane pilot of a commercial single/twin engine.

SUMMARY
Graduate of the University of California, Irvine, with Bachelor of Arts degree in Economics. Supplemented a challenging academic program with sailing and flying. Received a Private Pilot license as a personal goal outside of school and college sailing.

EDUCATION
Aeronautical
- American Flyers, San Diego, California, Instrument Rating, October 1994.

- Sunrise Aviation, Orange County, California, Private Pilot's License, December 1993.

General
- University of California, Irvine
  B.A. Economics, June 1994.

HONORS
- Nominee, Scholar-Athlete, University of California, Irvine, 1994.

- Collegiate All-American sailor, 1994.

- Collegiate All-American sailor, 1993.

EXPERIENCE
Aeronautical
- 240 hours, much of it complex, including transcontinental flights.

- Working on commercial rating now.

General
- Represented USA at Japan/USA Goodwill Regatta, Tokyo, Japan, 1993.

- Sailing Coach, University High School, San Diego, CA, 1992 - 1994.

- Yacht racing clinic instructor for Haneohe Yacht Club, Oahu, Hawaii, 1992 - 1993.

HOWARD LUM

125 Apple Lane
Daytona Beach, FL 32015
(904)555-8875

OBJECTIVE	A position in residential or commercial construction.
EDUCATION	Broward Community College, Fort Lauderdale, FL AA Landscape Architecture, 1994 GPA 2.94/4.00 Daytona Beach High School, Daytona Beach, FL Diploma, 1992 GPA 3.44/4.00
PART-TIME WORK EXPERIENCE	June to August, 1990 to 1993 Florida State Insulation Co. - Daytona Beach, FL Started as a laborer and worked up to the position of assistant foreman of a five-man crew. Responsible for previewing jobs, supplying material, and performing residential and commercial insulation applications. June to September, 1989 Simmons Roofing Company - Daytona Beach, FL Performed all phases of hot asphalt and shingle roofing on both commercial and residential properties.
PERSONAL	I am a very diligent and hard-working individual who has the ability to give and receive directions effectively. My hobbies include mountain climbing and skiing.
REFERENCES	Are available upon request.

MAXWELL Y. KITYAMA
4200 Birch Lane
Rome, GA 30163
(404)555-5450

OBJECTIVE

Full-time employment as a mechanic.

EXPERIENCE

BUTLER MACHINERY, Rome, GA   **Summers, 1991 to 1993**
Manufacturer of correct mechanical components for high technology.

Set up the operation of machine tools, including lathes, milling machines, drill presses, and grinders. Experienced with precision measuring instruments; fabrication procedures including welding, sheetmetal, and casting; and interpretation of documentation conventions for dimensions, tolerance, and finishing.

EDUCATION

Floyd College, Rome, GA
A.S. Mechanical Engineering, 1994

Rome High School, Rome, GA
Specialty - Mechanics, 1992

PERSONAL

I am skilled in mechanics, carpentry, masonry, painting, and landscaping.
I enjoy playing golf and baseball.
I am a volunteer coach for the local high school baseball summer league team.

REFERENCES

Full references will be furnished on request.

ROBERTO I. MARTINEZ

1690 Sandy Lane
Marianna, FL 34619
(813)555-7758

JOB OBJECTIVE

Technician/Assistant Engineer
Industrial/Production Electronics

A position offering upward mobility in a quiet, professional environment. I am confident I can adapt successfully to the industrial/production environment. I am a self-starter who will learn or re-learn whatever the position requires.

PART-TIME WORK EXPERIENCE

Summers, 1992 to 1993: **Marianna Radio/TV**, Marianna, FL
   TV, VCR, and Stereo Technician

Summer, 1991: **Allen TV Service**, Marianna, FL
   TV/Stereo Technician

Summer, 1990: **Wendy's**, Marianna, FL
   Food Server and Maintenance Worker

PERSONAL EVALUATION

I am an electronics technician with a strong background in repairing consumer electronic products. I have designed and breadboarded many electronic devices such as TTL circuits up to 14 ICs, audio special effects projects, laser and power supply projects, security systems, infrared and ultrasonic measuring tools, and surface mount technology projects.

EDUCATION

1994 Graduate of Chipola Junior College, Marianna, FL
   AA Equivalence certificates, Electronics, AC-DC, Semiconductors, Circuits, Digital Electronics 1-2, Microprocessors.

1992 Graduate of Marianna High School, Marianna, FL
   General Education

REFERENCES ON REQUEST

EMILIA E. ALDRICH

1609 Poppy Way
Franklin Springs, GA 30639
(404)555-0155

OBJECTIVE: A position in sales with opportunity to reach the managerial level.

PERSONAL: I always make an effort to complete scheduled projects successfully and on time.

I am eager to learn and attentive to quality.

I enjoy mountain biking, cooking, and fishing.

EXPERIENCE: **City Market**, Franklin Springs, GA.   Checker/Stock Clerk. Duties included ordering of groceries and supplies, stocking shelves, cashiering, making weekly deposits to checking account, recording and submitting welfare vouchers, and taking inventory. Summers, 1991, 1992, and 1993.

EDUCATION: 1994 Graduate of Emmanuel College, Franklin Springs, GA
     GPA 3.23/4.00
     Associate's degree in Business and Office Studies

1992 Graduate of Franklin Springs High School
     Educational focus on mechanics and business courses

REFERENCES: Available.

ROSAMARIA C. ALVAREZ
2550 Outlook Drive
Boise, ID 83725
(208)555-3242

OBJECTIVE:	A position as a senior or supervising receptionist providing efficient, high-quality typing, clerical, and word-processing services to a business firm.
EDUCATION:	Boise State University, Boise, ID Certificate in Business Practices, 1994 *Course Work*: • Typing: 70 WPM • Office Practice • Business Machines
EXPERIENCE:	**Manpower Temporary Services**, Boise, ID June to August, 1991, 1992, and 1993 *General Office Worker* • Filed applications, greeted applicants, and answered phones. • Assisted with administration and grading of applicants' tests, and completed all test paperwork. • Gained experience in light invoicing, setting up files, typing, and data entry. **Idaho State Automobile Association**, Boise, ID June to August, 1990 *Assistant Cashier, Relief PBX, and Relief DMV* • Assisted customers with paperwork. • Entered data in computer system.
COMPUTER EXPERIENCE:	• Excel • Lotus 1-2-3 • WordPerfect • Formtool • Norton Utilities • X-Tree
REFERENCES:	Available upon request.

CARRIE KING

704 Timberlake Court
Clinton, IA 52732
(319)555-1466

<u>Objective:</u>	A full-time position as clerical assistant with possibility of advancement.
<u>Education:</u>	Clinton Community College, Clinton, IA - 1994 Associate's degree, 1994
<u>Course Work:</u>	☐ WordPerfect 5.1 ☐ Lotus 1-2-3 ☐ Drafting ☐ Real Estate ☐ "Filing Efficiently" seminar ☐ "Take Charge Secretary" seminar
<u>Experience:</u>	AEC Communications, Clinton, IA *Part-time Receptionist.* 1991-1993 4 hours/day ☐ Greeted people and answered multi-lined telephone. ☐ Supported office staff. The Midwest Consumer, Clinton, IA *Personal Assistant.* Summer, 1990 ☐ Helped applicants and new employees with paperwork. ☐ Handled general office duties, including filing. ☐ Assisted payroll occasionally. ☐ Kept notes of committee meetings. ☐ Screened and interviewed applicants.

References will be provided upon request.

KEVIN R. LEE

46 LA MESA DRIVE   **COFFEYVILLE, KS 67337**   **(316)555-1058**

SUMMARY: Experienced in assembly of electro-mechanical devices pertinent to cathode ray tubes. Experienced with soldering, welding, cleaning, and leak-detection equipment. Familiar with most laboratory operations and tools including conformance to process specifications and collecting/organizing data.

EDUCATION:

11/93 - 11/94   Coffeyville Control Data Institute - Coffeyville, KS
Completed 853-hour course in computer technology. Studied basic and advanced electronics; digital logic and circuit analysis; Boolean algebra; CDC-Cyber 18-20 central processor; 8080 microprocessor; hardware and software; and peripheral equipment, including card equipment, line printer, magnetic tape transport and magnetic disc drive. Fifteen percent hands-on time. Course included extensive use of dual trace oscilloscope multimeter logic trainers and visual-display devices.

EXPERIENCE:

4/92 - 9/92   Mendelson Corporation - Coffeyville, KS
Test Technician
Tested and troubleshot a model 340 and a model 390 spectrophotometer. Performed tests on printed circuit boards and subassemblies.

Summers, 1990-91   Your Market - Coffeyville, KS
Checker/Stock Clerk
Ordered groceries and supplies, cashiered, made weekly deposits to checking account, took inventory, stocked shelves, recorded, and submitted food stamp vouchers.

REFERENCES: Available upon request.

Sophia L. Krook

Address:
746 Pineview Drive
Frederick, MD 21701
(301)555-3121

Objective:
To use my education and experience in a challenging position in computer-based technical or customer support, with potential for advancement.

Education:
George Washington University, Washington, D.C.
B.A. Anthropology, 1981, with emphasis in advertising
GPA 4.00/4.00

Frederick High School, MD
GPA 4.00/4.00
Graduated with highest academic honors, 1977

Awards:
1994 Matt Arnerich Community Service Award
George Washington University Honors, Outstanding Academic
    Achievement, 1981

**Skills and
Areas of Expertise:**
I have the ability to combine a high level of customer relations and organizational skills with a sound analytical knowledge of technical line production and troubleshooting; computer literate in production and diagnostic testing utilizing Hewlett Packard computers, frequency counters, spectrum analyzers, network analyzers, and power meters among others; self-taught PC familiarity and well-versed in DOS, skilled in Basic, Wordprocessing (Wordstar Pro, MS Word, Xedit, some Brief), database (dBase 3 Plus), communication protocols (Porcomm, Crosstalk, Relay Gold); also active on many bulletin boards and familiar with share ware and free ware in many categories.

References Available Upon Request

Sabrina K. Lara

40065 Early Way
Boise, ID 83725
(208)555-9203

Objective   A position as a personal office executive.

Education   Boise State University, 1980-1981
                     Nine Units toward Management Certificate
                     - Personnel Management
                     - Basic Supervision
                     - Computers in Management
                     Professional Office Training (14 units)
                     - Business English, Math, and Machines
                     - Office Procedures
                     - Refresher Typing and Shorthand
Other
                     Accounting Principles (6 units)
                     Seminars relating to the personnel field
                     - Wage and Salary Administration
                     - Hiring and Firing
                     - EEOC Compliance

Skills   Work well with people. Good writing and
                     organizational skills. Flexible and patient. Enjoy
                     creative projects.

Interests   Reading, music -- play flute and piano
                     Traveling and learning about other cultures

Experience   Self-Employed
                     Assist in the publication of a monthly newsletter,
                     The Quaker Trails and a quarterly one, Let's Talk
                     About Real Estate. Developed marketing materials
                     for a realtor including "Career Portfolio," and a
                     "Marketing Booklet" used to market individual
                     listings.

References will be provided upon request.

SIWA MSANGI

2590 Atlas Drive
Cedar Rapids, IA 52402
(319)555-5850

OBJECTIVE

Full-time executive secretary appointment with potential for advancement to personal assistant.

EDUCATION

Coe College - Cedar Rapids, IA
Bachelor of Arts, 1986
Major - Music
Minor - Art History and Appreciation
GPA 3.5/4.0

Cedar Rapids High School - 1982
Educational emphasis in theater and music

VOLUNTEER HISTORY

1987-1994   Des Moines Symphony Orchestra
                 Executive Secretary to President and Music Director

                 Provided administrative assistance. Prepared agendas and minutes of Board and Executive Committee meetings and scheduled meetings for fiscal year. Attended meetings for President; maintained business and social calendars Composed and transcribed correspondence. Supervised volunteers for special projects.

REFERENCES

Will be furnished upon request.

Brooke M. Dobos
1730 Cowper Street
Parsons, KS 67357
(913)555-9430

Objective: A position that will provide me opportunities to learn and progress.

Education: Labette Community College, Parsons, KS
Associate's degree in Computer and Information Sciences, 1988

Parsons High School, 1986

Skills and Experience:

Low Land Computer   1988-1994
As a volunteer in the family company, I became experienced in all aspects of the processing of domestic shipments.

o   Used U.P.S., Federal Express, and Airborne meter machines and Pitney Bowes U.S. Mail meter to dispatch and expedite truck shipments.

o   Processed international shipments.

o   Recorded and controlled all parts incoming and outgoing of the finished goods inventory.

o   Performed data entry, including Wordstar.

o   Recorded supplies used in the traffic department and created purchase orders.

McDonald's   Summers, 1985-1987
As opening cook, I became familiar with the process of making fast food.

o   Prepared food to order.

o   Restocked supplies to be used for the day.

References will be provided upon request.

LAURA KIRSTEN HUMMEL

529 PAUL REVERE DRIVE
LONGMEADOW, MA 01160
(413)555-3093

OBJECTIVE: A part-time job that will allow me to earn enough money to support myself for the next two years while attending culinary school.

EDUCATION: 1994 Graduate of Longmeadow High School
My scholastic GPA was 3.1/4.0

FUTURE PLANS: I will be attending Bay Path College for two years and working part-time. I then plan to attend a university and major in restaurant management.

EXPERIENCE: The past three summers I have worked at **Charlie's Deli Cafe** in Longmeadow, MA. My duties included taking food orders, checking stock, preparing food, and operating the cash register.

PERSONAL: I was a two-year member of Longmeadow High's German Club.

I was a cheerleader at Longmeadow High for four years.

I am hard-working and dedicated.

TRANSPORTATION: I own a 1984 Mazda truck that can be used for transportation and work if necessary.

REFERENCES: Jay Johnson, Teacher, Longmeadow High School, 555-0711.

Mary Hicks, Coach, Longmeadow High School, 555-0711.

Mitch L. DeLorenzo

29 Alta Drive
Fulton, MS 38843
(601)555-0331

Objective   I am very interested in obtaining employment that allows me to learn, move, and progress toward higher levels of performance. I am easily trained, a responsible employee, and a fun person to work with.

Education   I graduated from Fulton High School in 1994. My studies concentrated on economics and business.

I have always been very active in sports. While at Fulton High School, I participated on the following athletic teams:
      Soccer team (4 years; 2 years varsity).
      Track and cross-country team (3 years).
      Swim team (1 year).

I was the financial manager during my senior year of the varsity soccer team. This position taught me the importance of combining work and play.

I plan to attend Itawamba Community College for the next two years where my studies will focus on business economics.

Experience   Joseph's Motor Home Service and Repair, Fulton, MS
June 1, 1993 to September 1, 1993

I was responsible for washing and repairing recreational vehicles. My job also included installing new accessories and appliances in motor homes.

References   Joseph Goode
Joseph's Motor Home Service and Repair
555-8965

WILLIAM R. TANIMOTO
780 Weston Road
Mathiston, MS 39752
(601)555-4194

OBJECTIVE: A position as a part-time chef for the next two years with potential for full-time position after graduation from college.

EDUCATION: Graduate of Mathiston High School, 1994
GPA 2.80/4.00
I plan to attend Wood Junior College in Mathiston, MS during Fall 1995.

PERSONAL: Four-year member of the Mathiston High School baseball team.

Two-year member of the Adopt-a-Grandparent program at the Convalescent Hospital in Mathiston.

Reliable and ready to work.

EXPERIENCE:

Summers   **JACOB'S RIB COMPANY, Mathiston, MS**
1990-1994   **Cook and Food Preparations**

- Cooking
- Operating cash register
- Preparing food backups
- Bussing tables
- Counting the money in the cash register drawer

REFERENCES: Will be made available upon request.

REBECCA C. PALMER

ADDRESS

345 Kingsbury Drive
Hillsboro, MO 63050

TELEPHONE

(314)555-8832

PROFESSIONAL OBJECTIVE

A permanent position as a receptionist or secretary in a well-established company with good benefits and opportunities for advancement.

EDUCATION

Hillsboro High School - 1994

COURSE WORK

Shorthand	two semesters
Typing	two semesters
Record Keeping	one semester
Business Math	one semester

EXPERIENCE

Summer, 1994
Wendy's
Crew Person:
    Took customer orders
    Cooked
    Helped close the restaurant

REFERENCES

Available upon request.

CHRISTOPHER B. LASICA

398 MARION AVENUE
TARKIO, MO 64491
(816)555-5712

OBJECTIVE:

Permanent employment in the culinary industry, a position with possibility for advancement.

EDUCATION:

Poplar Bluff High School, Poplar Bluff, MO - 1994
Poplar Bluff Jr. High School - 1990
Poplar Bluff Elementary School - 1988

PERSONAL:

- Four-year member of Poplar Bluff High School's jazz choir.
- Four-year member of Poplar Bluff High School's performing band.
- Two-year member of Poplar Bluff High School's theater club.

EXPERIENCE:

Fry Cook	Panda Inn Poplar Bluff, MO	2/94 - 8/94
Waiter	Chef Tongs Poplar Bluff, MO	6/93 - 8/93
Cashier	Wells Pizza Poplar Bluff, MO	6/92 - 8/92

REFERENCES:

Will be made available upon request.

PAIGE MURTHA

308 MERIDITH AVENUE
MISSOULA, MT 59812
(406)555-3328

PROFESSIONAL OBJECTIVE

Employment as an aerobics instructor.

EDUCATIONAL BACKGROUND

1994 Graduate of Missoula High School.

RELEVANT COURSE WORK

Physical Education	4 semesters
Human Relations	1 semester
Psychology	1 semester
Physiology	1 semester

ACTIVITIES

Soccer	8 years
Swimming	4 years
Basketball	2 years
Softball	2 years
Soccer Team Manager	2 years

SUMMER EMPLOYMENT

1988 - 1994
YWCA Sports Camp, Missoula, MT

Head Counselor (1992-1994)
Responsible for children aged 6-12. Directed aerobics program.

Assistant Counselor (1988-1991)

REFERENCES

Available upon request.

JOHN NOWARK

217 Arthur Avenue
Omaha, NE 69337
(308)555-5003

Career Goal:	To secure a position as a nursery supervisor.
Education:	<u>Dundee High School</u> Graduate, 1994

General Education
GPA 3.00/4.00 overall, 3.50/4.00 science

Science Classes:

Horticulture	2 semesters
Biology	2 semesters

Art Courses:

Ceramics	1 semester
Basic Art, Drawing	1 semester

Mathematics:

Algebra	2 semesters
Geometry	2 semesters

Experience:

Summers, 1992 to 1994
<u>Sugar Hill Nursery</u>
453 Eureka Lane Omaha, NE 69337

Supervisor of Nursery - Stocked and supervised nursery plants.

Summers, 1990 to 1994
<u>4-H Camp</u>
1500 Eureka Lane Omaha, NE 69337

Counselor - Responsible for twenty children each year for one week in the month of July.

References:

Available upon request

CAROL M. LEE
1389 STEVENSON ROAD
DENVER, CO 80221
(303)555-1275

PROFESSIONAL OBJECTIVE
A position as a journalist in a firm with opportunities to use my writing skills.

EDUCATION
Graduate of Denver City High School - 1994
English Major
GPA: 4.00/4.00
English Courses:

    American Literature
    Composition 1
    Dreams and Myths
    Composition 2
    Short Story
    College English
    Shakespeare

EXPERIENCE
Golden Bear (school newspaper), Denver, CO

    Editor (1994)
    Reporter (1993)

The Coffee Pot, Denver, CO

    Administrative Assistant (3/92 to present)
    ◆   Handle accounts receivable and computer input, file, and type.

    Cashier (8/90 to 8/91)
    ◆   Waited on customers, answered phone, restocked shelves, and priced merchandise.

PERSONAL
Currently writing and self-publishing a collection of short stories about my family's heritage as pioneers.

REFERENCES
Furnished upon request.

NAME: **Matt J. Palmer**

ADDRESS: 254 Vista Oaks
                     Glendive, MT 59330

PHONE: (406)555-8427

OBJECTIVE: A position as an alarm technician in a firm with
                     opportunities for advancement.

EXPERIENCE: *Alarm Technician*
                     Primary Alarm
                     Part-time, 1991-1994

                     Installed alarms in large companies and residences.

EDUCATION: 1994 Graduate of Vista Oaks High School

                     Relevant Course Work:

Typing	2 semesters
Business Aide	2 semesters
Office Skills	2 semesters
Accounting	1 semester
Work Experience Ed.	3 semesters
Auto Shop	2 semesters

REFERENCES: Jack Siri
                     P.O. Box 578
                     Glendive, MT 59330
                     555-4308

                     Anne Osorio
                     687 Creek Drive
                     Lame Deer, MT 59101
                     555-3105

AARON C. KASAPI

276 Brooktree Ranch Rd.
Trinidad, CO 81082
(719)555-9335

Professional Objective:	A position in architectural drafting with a construction company.
Education:	Trinidad Public High School, 1993-1994 Graduate 1994 Stevenson High School, 1990-1993

Relevant Course Work:

Woodshop	3 years
Mechanical Drafting	1 year
Math	3 years
Architectural Drafting	2 years
Biology	1 year

School Sports:

Wrestling	4 years
Soccer	2 years
Football	1 year

Hobbies:
Creating computer graphics
Painting watercolors
Writing

Affiliations:
`Out to Lunch Gang` - a band that played music during lunchtime at high school.

Work Experience:

6/94-8/94
Mountain Adventures, Boulder, CO
Assistant Guide

Helped tourists manage horses, raised tents, and assisted in meal preparation.

6/93-8/93
Taco Bell, Trinidad, CO
Crew Member

Prepared food and cleaned restaurant.

References:
Will be made available upon request.

SELENA L. SHEN
198 Lake Drive
Manchester, CT 06040
(203)555-0304

POSITION DESIRED	Restaurant cashier or hostess
EDUCATION	Manchester High School Graduate, 1994 GPA 3.24/4.00
WORK EXPERIENCE	**Waterbury Restaurant**, Manchester, CT *Title*: Salad-maker *Duties*: Prepared salads and appetizers. *Supervisor*: Randy O'Neill *Dates*: July to September, 1993 **Straw Hat Pizza**, Manchester, CT *Title*: Hostess, Cashier, Waitress, Bus-person *Duties*: Greeted customers, managed customer seating, answered phone and took orders to go, operated a cash register and handled customer's money, served food, cleared tables, prepared salad bar, assisted in cooking of pizzas, and performed minimal maintenance chores. *Supervisor*: Marc Richards *Dates*: August 1992 to May 1993
ACTIVITIES	President, Manchester Scholarship Federation Member, Block A Club Member, Ski Gulls Club Member, volleyball and basketball teams
VOLUNTEER WORK	**Manchester Community Blood Bank** *Title:* Assistant *Duties:* Comforted blood donors, served refreshments, and typed required donor forms.
INTERESTS	Working with people in a social atmosphere Personal physical development program
REFERENCES	Available upon request.

JANICE E. KAHN
1005 Margaret Street
Willimantic, CT 06226
(203)555-9203

Objective   Part-time position as a gardener while I
attend Eastern Connecticut State University.

**Schools
Attended**   1994 Graduate of Willimantic High School
GPA 3.50/4.00

**Academic
Plans**   To attend Eastern Connecticut State University
in the fall of 1994 and major in botany.

**Specialty
Classes**   Regional Occupational Program course of
Horticulture

Human Relations	1 semester
Spanish	2 years
Biology	2 years
Typing	30 wpm

**Community
Activities**   Volunteer at the Mid-County Children's Center

**Hobbies and
Interests**   Playing the piano, gardening, cross-breeding
flowers, nature, running, and bicycling

**Work
Experience**   **Magic Farms Nursery**
June to August, 1991 - 1993
354 Floral Lane, Willimantic, CT 06226
Laborer - Packed and planted sprouts, changed
and lifted racks, planted bulk, and filled
and emptied sprout bins.

Part-time housecleaning
1989 - 1991

References   Will be made available upon request.

Douglas P. Shaw
191 Cuesta Way
Boise, ID 83706
(208)555-8599

Objective
A position in the field of graphic arts or as a photographer.

Education
Capitol High School, Boise, ID
Expected graduation date: 1994

Work Experience
Precious Moments Photography, Boise, ID
Photographic Assistant
Weekends 1990 to 1994
- Set up the lights and cameras
- Mixed chemicals
- Developed film and printed photographs

Jake's Chevron Station, Boise, ID
Daytime Laborer
Summers 1992 and 1993
- Handled two cash drawers, pumped gas, and made minor repairs
- Responsible for all bookkeeping on my shifts
- Kept garage area clean

Activities
Yearbook photography editor, 1994
Yearbook head photographer, 1993
Member, varsity soccer team, 1994
Member, junior varsity soccer team, 1993, 1992

Special Skills
Photography
Dependability
Punctuality
Making strangers feel comfortable

References will be made available upon your request.

JASON K. FARROW

462 Los Altos
Rexburg, ID 83460
(208)555-9025

GOAL: To work as an assistant manager in a pizza restaurant.

EDUCATION: Rexburg High School
Expected graduation date: 1994

EXPERIENCE: MAMA'S PIZZA - Rexburg, ID
Summer afternoons
Part-time during the school year

Food Preparation, 1994
Wash dishes, bus tables, operate cash register, and make sandwiches.

Crew, 1992 and 1993
Made pizzas, bussed tables, washed dishes, operated the register, and served customers.

ACTIVITIES: RED CROSS - Rexburg, ID
Volunteer Worker, 1994

INTERESTS: Snow skiing, water skiing, camping, reading, hiking, and being outdoors.

REFERENCES: Furnished upon request.

Jeffery R. Chuang

331 Hames Road
Belleville, IL 62221
(618)555-5293

<u>Objective</u>	To become a professional mechanic.
<u>Education</u>	Belleville High School - 1994
<u>Relevant</u> <u>Course Work</u>	Mechanics 1 and 2 Auto Shop 2 semesters Accounting 2 semesters
<u>Experience</u>	Summer 1993 <u>Belleville Auto Body</u> *Apprentice Bodyman* Prepared cars for painting, fixed dents, dismantled and reassembled various parts of the vehicle, and washed cars. Summers 1990-1992 <u>Texaco</u> *Station Attendant* Responsible for checking engine fluids, balancing tires, pumping gas, and related work.
<u>Interests</u>	Bike riding Snow skiing Music
<u>Activities</u>	Drummer for "The Fighting Fleas"
<u>References</u>	Available upon request.

LISA P. CHINCHIOLO

237 HAMMAN DRIVE
CHICAGO, IL 60606
(312) 555-3368

OBJECTIVE: A part-time position in a florist shop.

EXPERIENCE:

1993 - 1994 THE BUD SHOP

- Made bouquets
- Cared for plants and fresh flowers
- Operated a cash register
- Interacted with customers

1990 - 1991 VALLEY RANCH HOMES

- Maintained plants for model homes

1987 - 1990 HOUSE AND LAWN CARE

- Did odd jobs for area houses
- Mowed and watered lawns
- Watched houses and pets
- Did some landscaping and painting

EDUCATION: Hamman High School, Chicago, IL
Expected graduation date: 1994
GPA 4.00/4.00

Plans include attending Harold
Washington College, Chicago, IL.

SCHOOL ACTIVITIES: Member of the Chicago Scholarship
Federation. Attended all meetings and
participated in activities.

Four-year member of the Horticulture
Club. Final year as President.

*ADDITIONAL
INFORMATION*: I have received only As in school, and
will graduate from Hamman High School as
valedictorian with honors in science.

REFERENCES WILL BE MADE AVAILABLE UPON YOUR REQUEST.

Joseph M. O'Connell

324 Encinal Avenue
Huntington, IN 46750
(219)555-7419

PROFESSIONAL OBJECTIVE: A position as a cashier/bagger with a company providing opportunities for advancement.

EXPERIENCE:

1994 ALBERTSON'S
145 Playa Boulevard
Huntington, IN 46750

My primary job was bagging, however, I also did some janitorial work.

6/92 to 9/92 PLAZA SHELL SERVICE
1872 41st Avenue
Huntington, IN 46750

My primary job was working as a cashier and completing the janitorial work.

EDUCATION: HUNTINGTON HIGH SCHOOL - Diploma, 1993

RELEVANT COURSE WORK:

Mathematics	4 semesters
Computer Programming	1 semester
World History	2 semesters
U.S. History	2 semesters
English	6 semesters

SCHOOL ACTIVITIES:
2-year member of the soccer team
2-year member of the basketball team
3-year member of the weight-lifting club

REFERENCES: Available on request.

Geoffery E. Pace
121 Corinne Avenue
Gary, IN 46408
(218)555-5452

Immediate Objective:	To gain a part-time position working with the environment. I seek a position that will enable me to attend the local community college and obtain my degree in ranger services.
Career Objective:	To become a forest ranger.
Previous Work Experience:	
6/94-8/94	Camp Carloads 1956 Vista Drive Gary, IN 46408 Dishwasher
1/94-5/94	Gary Radio 92 Hanger Way Gary, IN 46408 Phone Solicitor
8/92-10/93	Burger King Restaurant 1782 Freedom Drive Gary, IN 46408 Counter Worker
Education:	Gary High School, 1994 Gary, IN GPA 2.7/4.0
School Activities:	Member of the French club, 1994 Member of the jazz choir, 1991-1994 Member of the basketball team, 1993-1994
Additional Comments:	I have also done yard work, including pulling weeds, splitting and stacking wood, hauling brush, and cutting trees into manageable lengths. I especially enjoy being outdoors. I learn quickly and have a well-developed work ethic.
Personal References:	Available upon request.

KRISTY S. PACHECO
1834 Jennifer Drive
Murray, KY 42071
(502)555-0739

OBJECTIVE   To work for an executive who needs a full-time assistant to take over routine functions and detail work.

WORK EXPERIENCE

10-93 to present   Fantasy Cakes, Murray, KY
Position: Register and counter person
Duties: Clean, wait on customers, operate the cash register, and take cake orders.

7-92 to 10-92   Mickey's One Hour Photo, Murray, KY
Position: Counter person
Duties: Wait on customers, operate the cash register, develop negatives, and print pictures.

7-91 to 7-92   Pioneer Museum, Murray, KY
Position: Typist
Duties: Type manuscripts, lead tours, and mow lawns.

OTHER EXPERIENCE   President of high school student council
Basketball coach for junior high
Member of 4-H horse club

EDUCATION   Murray High School - 1994
GPA 3.57/4.00

**RELEVANT
COURSE WORK**

Typing	2 years	64 wpm
Accounting	1 semester	
Computer Literacy	1 semester	
Computer Programming	1 year	

REFERENCES   Will be available upon request.

GINA L. LASICA
571 Vienna Drive
Pikeville, KY 41501
(606)555-5941

OBJECTIVE:
To obtain an entry-level job in business with opportunity to enter management.

EDUCATION:
I am a recent graduate of Pikeville High School - 1994.
My grade point average was 3.85/4.00.

I have taken courses in word processing, accounting, and typing (40 wpm). I am literate with IBM and Apple computers.

WORK EXPERIENCE:
May 1992 - February 1993
Dick Bruhns
Pikeville, KY
Responsibilities: Assisted customers with purchases and operated cash register.

August 1991 - May 1992
Jacob's Drug Store
Pikeville, KY
Responsibilities: Wrapped customers' purchases, assisted customers, and operated cash register.

May - August 1991
Fischer Corporation
Pikeville, KY
Responsibilities: Worked on inventory and light bookkeeping.

EXTRACURRICULAR:
Member of student government, 1992,1994
Member of yearbook staff, 1993,1994
Member of volleyball team, 1991-1994

REFERENCES:
Available upon request.

ADAM E. QUAN

571 Miller Court   Slidell, LA 70460   (504)555-1809

OBJECTIVE   To utilize my organizational and analytical skills in the
                 financial industry while I continue my education toward a
                 career as a Certified Public Accountant.

EDUCATION   Slidell High School - 1994

                 In 1994, I will attend Grambling State University in
                 Grambling, LA. I plan to receive my Bachelor's degree
                 in Accounting in 1998.

EMPLOYMENT
November 1993 to June 1994
        Dave's Deli Restaurant, Slidell, LA.

        *   Managed cash receipts and cash flow of customers'
                activity through cashiering duties.
        *   Maintained good customer relations through hosting.
        *   Provided clean work areas by bussing work stations.

June 1993 to September 1993
        The Lodge, Slidell, LA.

        *   Handled the opening and closing procedures of both the
                restaurant and store facility.
        *   Responsible for customer service, which included
                cashiering, bussing work stations, and hosting.

November 1992 to June 1992
        Dave's Deli Restaurant, Slidell, LA.

        *   Learned how to manage cash transactions through
                training in cash register use.
        *   Operated client payment transactions via cashiering.
        *   Trained in the importance of customer relations through
                hosting.

REFERENCES AVAILABLE UPON REQUEST

PABLO A. RAMIREZ

261 Baltusrol Way
Baton Rouge, LA 70803
(504)555-5069

Job Goal

A permanent part-time position as a salesperson
and cashier.

Education

Central High School - 1993
143 Central Street, Baton Rouge, LA 70803
Course work for a business major:
     Accounting
     Economics
     Psychology

School Activities

Four-year member of football team
Four-year member of S.A.D.D. (Students Against
     Drunk Driving)
Three-year member of the Business Club
     Final year I served as president

Work Experience

Blockbuster Video
435 Desilva Street
Baton Rouge, LA 70803
Duties: sales and cashier

Sidney's Food Store
200 Desilva Street
Baton Rouge, LA 70803
Duties: sales, cashier, and telephone

Personal Statement

I am a warm, sincere person who is eager to learn
and willing to work hard.

References Available Upon Request

<u>Name</u>	**JAMES C. RICHARDS**
<u>Address</u>	1740 Webster Woods Drive Lake Charles, LA 70609 (318)555-2347
<u>Career Objective</u>	A position in business management in which I can use my skills in the areas of strategic management, business research, and consistent management.
<u>Education</u>	Lake Charles High School Graduate, 1993 GPA 3.4/4.0
<u>Relevant Courses</u>	Advanced Math History English Foreign Language, French

<u>Work History</u>

Hughes Union 76
Lake Charles, LA
April 1993 to September 1993

<u>Station Attendant</u>
Duties: Helped customers at the full-service island and at the self-service island. Did minor mechanical repairs: radiator hoses, tires, batteries, and belts. This job indicates my ability to work with demanding and frustrated customers in pressure situations.

The Tribune (newspaper)
Lake Charles, LA
March 1993 to April 1993

<u>Paper Inserter</u>
Duties: Began work at 12:00 AM and prepared newspapers for delivery. The job was usually completed in four hours. This job indicates my ability to work diligently regardless of time of day.

<u>References</u>   Available upon request.

LAURA T. HOLDAWAY

576 Mesquite Drive
Waterville, ME 04901
(207)555-8458

OBJECTIVE

To find a job that calls for learning and creativity and offers advancement in a friendly, people-oriented atmosphere.

EDUCATION

1993 Graduate of Waterville High School in Waterville, ME
Grade Point Average 3.64/4.00

Relevant Course Work:
    Biology
    U.S. Government
    American Literature

WORK EXPERIENCE

The King's Service
Cleaning Service
July 1993

Clerical Worker: Typed up work orders, filed, and answered business telephone.

The Perfect Place
Clothing Store
March 1993

Sales Clerk: Sold clothing during side-walk sales.

Floral Furnishings
Wholesale Florist Supply
1992 to 1993

Clerical Worker: Wrote orders, did stock control, filed business papers, and answered business telephone.

REFERENCES AVAILABLE UPON REQUEST

FRANCINE P. SMITH

786 Quartz Street
Bangor, ME 04401
(207)555-8692

Occupational Goal:	I would eventually like to become a dietician. Presently, I am seeking a part-time job that will allow me to attend school to learn about my chosen field.
Education:	High School: Bangor High School Degree: High school diploma, 1994 Grade average: A-/B+
Special Skills:	I learn rapidly and work well with other people.
Hobbies:	Exercising Skiing Socializing
Activities:	Member of the Bangor High School Key Club and American Field Service during my junior year. Member of the Bangor High School Concert and Marching Band during my freshman year.

Work Experience:

6/94 - 9/94	Child-care provider for fifteen hours a week.
9/93 - 5/94	House cleaner for three to four hours per week.
6/92 - 8/93	Babysitter and house cleaner for four to five hours a week.
References:	Available upon request.

NICOLA E. RHODES

938 INDIANA AVENUE
AUGUSTA, ME 04330
(207)555-5809

OBJECTIVE

To obtain a part-time position with a firm whose focus is public relations. The position should lead to a full-time position after graduation from college.

EDUCATION

1994 Student at Farmington University
Business and French major

1993 Graduate of Augusta High School
GPA 3.8/4.0

SPECIAL ABILITIES AND STUDIES

I have taken advanced courses in math and trigonometry, English literature, business, science, and computer technology and programming.

I speak fluent French.

I am experienced with a computerized cash register.

PREVIOUS EMPLOYMENT

Burger King Restaurant
200 Main Street, Augusta, ME
September 1993 to January 1994

Duties: Cashier (computerized)
             Food preparation
             Dishwasher

REFERENCES AVAILABLE UPON REQUEST

ANGELA T. SANCHEZ

301 Coates Way
Alpena, MI 49707
(517)555-8104

Objective: Part-time position in communications that would utilize my past experiences while enabling me to continue my studies at Andrews University in Berrien Springs, MI. Position should include promotional possibilities.

Education: Alpena High School, 1993
I will attend Andrews University beginning in the fall of 1994. I plan to receive my Bachelor's degree in Communications in 1998.

Work Experience:

June 1993 to
Present

Customer Relations/Secretary
Jim's Audio Video Service Co.

Responsibilities: helping customers, filing, answering phones, ordering parts, and recording accounts payable and accounts receivable.

August 1992

Researcher
Supervisorial Campaign Committee

Responsibilities: performing microfilm research.

June 1991 to
August 1991

Office Assistant
Alpena Board of Realtors

Responsibilities: putting together and mailing newsletters, filing, and typing.

Other Experience: Member of varsity tennis and softball teams, 1992-1993.
Member of yearbook staff - reporter and layout designer, 1992-1993.
Member of Michigan Scholarship Association, 1992-1993.
Proficient in Spanish.

References: Available upon request.

CHRISTIANNA M. NELSON

900 Bear Valley Drive   Escanaba, MI 49829   (906)555-2380

IMMEDIATE OBJECTIVE
To obtain a position as an assistant physical therapist enabling me to work with physically disabled individuals while I attend college. I would prefer employment with a company that would place me in a permanent physical therapist position once I have graduated from college.

LONG-TERM OBJECTIVE
To become a physical therapist.

EDUCATION
Escanaba High School in Escanaba, MI - 1993
GPA 3.9/4.0

My educational plans are to attend Calvin College in Grand Rapids, MI. I plan to major in education of the physically handicapped.

ACADEMIC ACTIVITIES
I was a member of the high school Interact Club (a Community Service Organization) for four years. I was president of the club my senior year.

EMPLOYMENT HISTORY
Summers 1992, 1993   BAY DE NOC CAMP, Madison, WI

Camp Counselor for developmentally disabled teenagers and adults.

Academic 1991, 1992, 1993   ESCANABA HIGH SCHOOL, Escanaba, MI

Volunteer Aid to Special Education teacher.

REFERENCES AVAILABLE UPON REQUEST.

AMANDA CAINE
732 Strathmore Ave.
Los Angeles, CA 90024
(310)555-0945

OBJECTIVE   A financial analyst position that utilizes my skills and experience.

EDUCATION

1990-1994   **University of California, Los Angeles**
Bachelor's degree in Economics and Anthropology. Course work includes calculus, corporate finance, statistics, and English.

1993   **UCLA in France**, Paris, France
Studied art, history, language, and culture of France.

EXPERIENCE

Summer, 1993   **Joseph Brothers**
New York,NY
Analyst
Analyzed real estate markets and properties. Drafted and researched marketing materials for sale of properties. Derived cash flow projections and analyzed structuring alternatives for sale of a retail center.

Summer, 1992   **University of California Library System**
Los Angeles, CA
Library Assistant
Sorted and alphabetized daily charges and discharges into filing system. Attended to customers' needs at the loan desk.

Summers, 1991 and 1990   **Monte Vista Tennis Club**
Los Angeles, CA
Tennis Instructor
Developed and managed a tennis program for pupils of different ages and skill levels at a community facility. Marketed the program by distributing flyers door-to-door. Hired two tennis instructors because of program's growth.

References available upon request.

Joshua K. Peck
301 Coates Drive
International Falls, MN 56649
(218)555-2452

Objective: To become an actor in a community theater.

Acting Experience: Member of the Drama Club for four years.

Acted in "The People vs Maxine Loe," my senior year in High School.

Work Experience:
June 1993   McDonald's Restaurant
to Present   International Falls, MN

Responsibilities: operate cash register, improve and maintain the site and lobby, make fries, cook the food, and close the restaurant at night.

June 1992   Taco Bell Restaurant
to August 1992   International Falls, MN

Responsibilities: operated electronic cash register, prepared and packaged the food, and cleaned and maintained restaurant.

Personal: Competed in track and field for six years. I was a multi-event winner and team captain my senior year.

Member of the football team for two years: 1992, 1993.

Fluent in written and conversational French.

Education: Graduated from International Falls High School in 1993

Social Studies award winner.

Plan to attend St. Cloud State University in St. Cloud, MN in 1994. I will major in Speech/Communication/Theater Education and will graduate in 1998.

References: Available upon request.

HANK MADRUGA

243 Shoreview Way
Minneapolis, MN 55454
(612)555-7080

OBJECTIVE

To write for a trade journal or house publication.

WORK EXPERIENCE

December 1993 - present:

Pete's Deli-Cafe
Minneapolis, MN

General help responsible for operating cash register, taking food orders, doing dishes, making decisions concerning supplies, catering, stocking supplies, dealing with the public, and preparing some food.

Prior to December 1993:

Miscellaneous Jobs

Housecleaned, baby-sat, gardened, and cashiered at a bookstore.

OTHER EXPERIENCE

- Member, Lakeside High School newspaper staff
- Member, Lakeside High School ski club
- Member, Lakeside High School baseball team
- Member, Lakeside High School swim team
- Member, Lakeside High School track and field team
- Member, Lakeside High School cross-country team

EDUCATION

Lakeside High School, Minneapolis, MN, 1993
GPA 2.8/4.0

REFERENCES

Will be made available upon your request.

TRINA W. PERFUMO

236 QUAIL RUN
DENVER, CO 80222
(303)555-1498

OBJECTIVE:

To become a professional ski instructor.

WORK EXPERIENCE:

	Ski Lift Operator, Ski Instructor
Winters, 1992, 1993, 1994	Hesperus Ski Area, Durango, CO

Worked lifts, reported problems, taught children and adults how to ski.

	Bus Boy, Food Preparer
June 1993 to August 1993	The Wild Side Cafe, Durango, CO

Bussed tables, washed dishes, and prepared food for the next day.

OTHER EXPERIENCE:

Member of Durango Ski Rescue Team, 1994
Member of high school ski team, 1991-1994
Member of Denver CO Youth Group, 1992

EDUCATION:

1994 Graduate of Roosevelt High School
Denver, CO

REFERENCES:

References will be furnished upon request.

Frank P. Reyes

988 El Sereno Court
Stratham, NH 03885
(603)555-1798

OBJECTIVE

To work as a part-time chef while I attend classes at New Hampshire Technical College in Stratham, NH. The job should include the possibility of promotion and a full-time position after I graduate from college.

EDUCATION

Stratham High School, Stratham, NH
General Studies Diploma, 1994
GPA 2.9/4.0
Relevant Course Work:

Cooking	two semesters
Nutrition	two semesters
Food Chemistry	two semesters
English	four years
French	four years

WORK EXPERIENCE

June 1993 to August 1993
Food Service Worker
Rudolph's Restaurant
267 Lahai Roi Street, Stratham, NH 03855
<u>Responsibilities</u>: Preparing food for the next day, operating the cash register, and cooking.

June 1992 to August 1992
Food Service Worker
Dairy Queen
489 Cross Street, Stratham, NH 03855
<u>Responsibilities</u>: Managing cash flow, acting as night manager occasionally, operating the cash register, cooking, and preparing food.

REFERENCES WILL BE MADE AVAILABLE UPON YOUR REQUEST.

Elly G. Minch

245 Chaparral Drive
Chester, NH 03036
(603)555-1364

Objective:

To secure a part-time job as a cashier that will enable me to attend classes while earning money to pay for my college education.

Education:

Chester High School - 1993
764 Chaparral Drive
Chester, NH 03036
GPA 3.5/4.0

I will be attending Notre Dame College, Manchester, NH, in the fall of 1993. I plan to major in psychology.

School Activities and Course Work:

Business Education - 2 semesters

Top secretarial typist - 4 years of typing. Helped teach other classmates how to type.

Varsity swim team member for 3 years - school's top swimmer

Work Experience:

June to August, 1993   Cashier (part-time)
Baskin Robbins - ice cream parlor
Opened store on weekends and handled some bookkeeping.

June to August, 1992   Cashier (part-time)
Candy's Kitchen - restaurant

References:

Available upon request

EMANUEL R. MARTINEZ

234 Kingsbury Drive, Auburn, NY 13021
(315)555-6757

Objective: To secure part-time employment in the field of business management while I continue my education.

Education: Auburn High School - 1993
GPA - 3.8/4.0

Next year I will attend Canisius College in Buffalo, NY. I plan to major in business administration and management. I will graduate in 1997.

Activities:
- Volunteer food server at Friday's Food Center for the homeless twice a month.
- Four-year member of the Auburn High School speech group, Junior Statesmen of America.
- Four-year member of the Auburn High School Varsity Football Team, team captain senior year.

Work Experience:

June to August 1991, 1992, 1993
Salesman, Delivery Driver, Cashier
The One Stop Shop, Auburn, NY
I started by merchandising, graduated to cashier, and was promoted to delivery driver.

Special Skills: Built and sold furniture; designed and constructed promotional signs and merchandise displays; learned the workings of shipping and receiving departments; trained personnel for all jobs mentioned above.

General: I am a creative worker who is artistically inclined. I can do challenging jobs both thoroughly and efficiently. I am communicative with the public as well as with my fellow employees. I am capable of sticking with a job, as is shown by my work experience.

References: Will be available when requested.

KIMBERELY C. BAKER
456 BALTUSROL WAY
TARBORO, NC 27886
(919)555-0922

OBJECTIVE

A part-time job as a receptionist for a company which provides the possibility of promotion into business management.

EDUCATION

1993 Tarboro High School
GPA 3.20/4.00

My educational plans are to attend **Edgecombe Community College** in Tarboro, NC, full time for the next two years. I will transfer to **East Carolina University** in Greenville, NC, to obtain my bachelor's degree in business administration and management.

EXPERIENCE

RECEPTIONIST
Leon T. Beacom, CPA
Tarboro, NC
Summers 1992 and 1993

Responsibilities: Answering phones, filing papers, and making business appointments.

SCOREKEEPER
Tarboro Youth Basketball Association
Tarboro, NC
November to February 1991, 1992, and 1993

Responsibilities: Writing score sheets, recording the score, and reporting score results to the newspaper.

OTHER EXPERIENCE

o Member of Student Government at Tarboro High for 3 years. Associated Student Body President senior year.
o Member of the Tarboro High varsity basketball team for 3 years. Played junior varsity basketball for 1 year.
o Member of the Tarboro High varsity softball team for 3 years.
o Member of Tarboro High varsity track for one year.
o Member of Tarboro High SADD (Students Against Drunk Driving) club.
o Worked at the Special Olympics for 2 years.

REFERENCES UPON REQUEST

Tracey Warrick
467 Altivo Drive
Yellow Springs, OH 45387
(513)555-1875

Objective: To serve as a part-time travel agent in a firm that provides
                    the possibility of advancement and a full-time position
                    once I have finished college.

Work Experience: June 1994 to present
                    Word Processor, Data Entry
                    The Book Worm, Yellow Springs, OH
                    Responsibilities: Answering correspondence, entering data
                    including account receivables, and mailing information.

                    Prior to June 1994
                    Miscellaneous jobs such as baby-sitting, housesitting, and
                    housecleaning.

Other Experience:

            o   Competitive Swimming: My participation with the
                    Yellow Springs High School swim team and the Aqua
                    Devils swim team has increased my ability to handle
                    competition and stress.

            o   Leadership: I was in charge of the operation of the
                    Yellow Springs High School Blood Bank for two years.

            o   Travel: I am experienced in many different kinds of
                    travel including camping, backpacking, and canoeing.

Education: 1994 Graduate of Yellow Springs High School
                    GPA 2.6/4.0

            o   I am currently enrolled in two night courses focused on
                    the travel agency business: Regional Occupational
                    Program and a computer course on the Apollo series
                    working with the computerized OAG.

            o   My educational plans are to major in communications and
                    to graduate from Antioch College in Yellow Springs, OH
                    in 1998.

References available upon request.

Kelly I. McGee

5640 Los Altos Blvd.
Shawnee, OK 74801
(405)555-7694

Objective:	Part-time position with an accounting firm that has the potential to offer a full-time position in four years upon my completion of college.
Work Experience:	

June 1993 to August 1993	Salesperson
	Sears Roebuck, Shawnee, OK
	Responsibilities:
	    Stocking and straightening merchandise
	    Assisting customers
	    Ordering draperies
	    Answering phones
	    Operating cash register

Prior to June 1993	Miscellaneous jobs such as baby-sitting and gardening.
Other Abilities:	Basic accounting skills Type 50 words per minute Speak some Spanish

Education:	Shawnee High School
	GPA 3.3/4.0
	Applicable course work:
	    Accounting 1 & 2
	    Advanced Accounting
	    English 1 - 4
	    Mathematics through Pre-Calculus
	Next year I will attend Oklahoma State University in Stillwater, OK. I will major in accounting and anticipate graduating with a bachelor's degree in 1997.

Activities:	Four-year member of the Shawnee High School Marching Band. I was trombone player. Two-year member of the Shawnee High School Business Club. I was club president my senior year.

References:	Sam Ely, Shawnee High School Teacher, 555-0880
	    Mathematics
	Joan Lazo, Shawnee High School Teacher, 555-0880
	    Accounting

CAROL M. LOOMIS

85 Peace Drive
Portland, OR 97219
(503)555-0186

OBJECTIVE: A part-time position as a dance instructor that will enable me to attend classes while working with children.

EDUCATION: June 1994 Graduate of Lakeside High School
Portland, OR
GPA 3.00/4.00

In Fall 1994, I will attend Lewis and Clark College in Portland, OR. I will graduate in 1998 with a Bachelor's degree in Dramatic Arts.

WORK EXPERIENCE: Assistant Dance Instructor
The Dance Studio, Portland, OR

Responsibilities: teaching tap and jazz to school-aged children.
Summers 1992, 1993

SPECIAL SKILLS: Two-year member of 4-H club
Four years jazzercize
Six years tap and ballet lessons
I am a very diligent and friendly dance instructor

REFERENCES: Cathy Delude, dance instructor, The Dance Studio
555-1154
Norman Haney, family friend
555-7600

Nathaniel J. Abreo

4322 Clares Street
Butler, PA 16003
(412)555-6897

OBJECTIVE

To obtain a part-time position with an architectural firm that will enable me to gain experience in the field of architecture. The position should provide the possibility for advancement with the completion of my scholastic studies.

EDUCATION

Butler High School, Butler, PA, 1993
Graduated in the top 20% of class
GPA: 3.2/4.0
Next year I will attend Butler County Community College where I plan to major in architecture.

WORK EXPERIENCE

Food Service Worker   June 1993 to August 1993

McDonald's Restaurant, Butler, PA
Responsible for taking and preparing food orders, operating the cash register, preparing food, cleaning lobby and food area, and stocking supplies.

General Worker   Prior to June 1993

Miscellaneous Jobs
Performed baby-sitting and gardening tasks.

OTHER EXPERIENCE

Member of Butler High Varsity Tennis team
Proficient in German
Active member of the Boys Club of Butler

References available upon request

MORGAN A. WRIGHT

896 Mesa Drive
Columbia, SC 29208
(803)555-4079

OBJECTIVE	To become an agent in a real estate agency.
WORK EXPERIENCE	**Columbia Pizza Company, Columbia, SC**
	Dough Roller
	Responsibilities:
	Providing a clean work area
	Flouring the table
	Rolling and cutting the dough
	Mixing the dough batch for the following day
	The Supreme Pizza, Columbia, SC
	Bus Boy
	Responsibilities:
	Completing "prep list"
	Collecting dishes
	Putting dishes away
	Cleaning restaurant and closing-up
OTHER EXPERIENCE	Member of DeYoung High School Jazz Band
	Sold candy for a school fundraiser
EDUCATION	Recent graduate of DeYoung High School
	Columbia, SC
	GPA: 2.5/4.0

Full references will be provided on request.

AMY J. FENNELL

445 Polo Drive
Portland, OR 97201
(503)555-1967

OBJECTIVE

To be a fashion designer

EDUCATION

High School: *Upland High School*
Degree: *High school diploma - 1993*
Grade Average: *B*
In the fall of 1993 I will attend Bassist College in
Portland, OR where I plan to receive an Associate
degree in fashion design.

ACTIVITIES

My junior year I helped start a new group at Upland
High School called S.A.D.D. (Students Against Drunk
Driving). I was the group's treasurer my senior year.

I was a member of Junior Statesmen of America (JSA)
my junior and senior years.

My sophomore and junior years, I kept statistics for the
junior varsity basketball team.

During my freshman year, I kept statistics for the
freshman basketball team.

WORK EXPERIENCE

Miscellaneous jobs such as lawn mowing and baby-
sitting.

References will be provided upon your request.

Johnny K. Litchfield

452 Baja Sol Drive
Sioux Falls, SD 57197
(605)555-9506

Objective:	A permanent position as a carpenter.
Work Experience:	Jack's Pizza
Sioux Falls, SD
Dishwasher
Period of Service: 4 months
Education:	1993 Graduate of Sioux Falls High School
Grade Average B-

| | Relevant Courses: | Construction I,II
Mechanical Drawing |
|---|---|---|

Special Skills:	Woodworking	Three years
	Landscaping	One year in home garden
	Bassist	Currently preforming in a band

References:	Jack Core	Richard Crivello
	Owner Jack's Pizza	Family Friend
	555-0793	555-3702

DEBBIE R. NEWELL
2986 Middle Avenue
Rapid City, SC 57701
(605)555-1307

OBJECTIVE:

Full-time employment as a secretary while I attend night classes.

PARTICULARS:

*   Typing   75 wpm

*   WordPerfect, Word

*   Lotus 1-2-3, Quattro Pro, Quicken

EDUCATION:

Rapid City High School, Rapid City, SC
Degree: 1994 General Studies

I will attend Western Dakota Vocational Technical Institute for two years beginning in the fall of 1994.

WORK EXPERIENCE:

K-mart
Clerk - women's clothing department
Cash Register Operator
9/92 to present
Full-time during the summer
Part-time during the academic year

EXTRACURRICULAR:

*   Member of the high school choir and jazz choir.

*   Participated in Girl Scout activities for 3 years.

*   Served as a camp counselor for Brownies and Pixies at the City Park.

REFERENCES:

Available upon your request.

ANGELA R. CHACON

564 Meadowview Court
Castleton, VT 05735
(802)555-8102

OBJECTIVE

To work in the art/graphic design department of an advertising agency.

WORK EXPERIENCE

Customer Relations/Secretary
Designs Unlimited
Castleton, VT
June to August, 1994

Office Assistant
Penn Ad Agency
Castleton, VT
June to August, 1993

Baby-sitting
Prior to June, 1993

OTHER EXPERIENCE

Member of yearbook staff, 1993-1994
Member of Castleton Scholarship Federation, 1993-1994
Member of varsity tennis and softball teams, 1992-1994
Fluent in Spanish

EDUCATION

I graduated from Castleton High School in June 1994. My educational
plans are to attend Castleton State College in Castleton, VT. I plan to
major in drawing and fine arts.

REFERENCES

Will be provided upon your request.

NAME: **Carla Grant**

ADDRESS: 2976 Lucky Lane
                         Cleveland, TN 37320

TELEPHONE: (615)555-1745

OBJECTIVE: Part-time position in a clothing goods
                         store as a register operator or sales
                         clerk.

EDUCATION: Knoxville High School, 1994
                         Knoxville, TN
                         GPA 3.0/4.0
                         My educational plans are to attend
                         Cleveland State Community College in
                         Cleveland, TN. I will major in marketing
                         and sales.

EXPERIENCE: JCPenney
                         May 1994 to present
                               Cash register operator

                         The Emporium
                         January 1992 to November 1993
                               Sales clerk

EXTRACURRICULAR: •   Junior Achievement, 1993, 1994
                         •   Member of Zenith Group (a public
                               speaking club), 1994
                         •   Sophomore Magazine Sales - Class
                               Coordinator, 1992

QUALIFICATIONS: I am a committed, hardworking, and punctual
                         employee who interacts skillfully with
                         customers.

REFERENCES: Kay Dietze, Junior Achievement Sponsor
                         (615)555-2778

                         Linda Nealis, JCPenney, (615)555-4410

Kyle J. Ahn

589 Bavington Drive
Nashville, TN 37209
(615)555-4589

Objective

Full-time employment in the field of business management.

Work Experience

Kroger
Nashville, TN
Position: Courtesy Clerk
Responsibilities: Bagging groceries, serving customers, and maintaining site.
June to August, 1994

The Fish Bowl Pet Center
Nashville, TN
Position: Assistant Manager
Responsibilities: Selling, maintaining shop, ordering supplies, closing out register, opening and closing the store.
June to August, 1993

Other Experience

Auto-mechanics
Drafting
Woodwork

Education

Graduate of Memorial High School - 1994
GPA: 2.75/4.00
Four-year member of boy's volleyball team
Four-year member of Business Club

My future educational goals are to attend Nashville State Technical Institute part time, majoring in business. I plan to work full time while attending college.

References

Peter Lane, Owner, The Fish Bowl, 555-0765
Donna Staley, Neighbor, 555-1365
Ron Nix, Family Friend, 555-5502

LEON C. CARLOS

290 Hampshire Road
Provo, UT 84602
(901)555-1834

Objective   Part-time position with a company in the field of business and management.

Work Experience

June 1994 to August 1994   Arco Station
                                  Provo, UT
                                  Station Attendant
                                  Responsibilities: Operating cash register, light stocking, and cleaning.

March 1994 to June 1994   The Water Hole
                                  Provo, UT
                                  Swim School Maintenance
                                  Responsibilities: Add chlorine as necessary. Clean and vacuum pool.

Prior to March 1994   Woodland Timber
                                  Wood Cutter and Splitter
                                  Provo, UT
                                  Responsibilities: Cut, split, and hauled wood for personal use and profit.

Other Experience

- Experienced in fiberglass repair.
- Member of Utah Scholarship Federation - 4 years.
- Member of varsity soccer team - 2 years. Team captain senior year.
- Member of junior varsity soccer team. Received valuable player award - 1992.
- Fluent in Spanish.
- Three-year member of Big Brother, Big Sister program.

Education

1994 Graduate of Provo High School
- GPA 3.1/4.0
- My educational plans are to attend Brigham Young University, in Provo, UT. My degree objective is to obtain a B.A. in business.

References will be provided upon your request.

Dale Crivello

257 Huntington Drive
Middlebury, VT 05753
(802)555-4294

Objective:	Part-time position as a chef or assistant chef providing the opportunity of advancement upon my graduation from college.

Education: Middlebury High School
- Expected graduation date: 1994
- GPA: 3.5/4.0
- Relevant course work:
  Mathematics through Geometry
  Home Economics 1 and 2
  Human Nutrition
  2 years of French
- I will attend New England Culinary Institute in Montpelier, VT in the fall. I will major in food production, management, and services.

Work Experience:

2/93 - 8/93   **Denny's Restaurant**
I was the preparation cook and enjoyed my job. Unfortunately, I had to quit my job when the football season started.

6/92 - 8/92   **Swensen's Ice Cream Factory**
I dipped cones and decorated various ice cream products.

Other Experience:

- Varsity football team, 4 years, MVP senior year
- Soccer league, 4 years
- Ski club, 4 years

References: Available on request.

ROGER NEWTON
765 Murphy's Lane
Arlington, VA 22207
(703)555-3099

OBJECTIVE:	To become a full-time auto mechanic.

EDUCATION:　　1994 Graduate of Arlington High School
GPA 2.5/4.0
Relevant Course Work:

Auto shop	2 years
Auto shop student supervisor	1 year
Business math	1 year

EXPERIENCE:

6/93 to present　　ARLINGTON SHELL, Arlington, VA
Station Attendant
Responsible for operating the cash register, assisting customers, checking oil, washing windows, checking tire pressure, and fixing flat tires.

Prior to 6/93　　ODD JOBS
Gardening, dog walking, catering, clean-up work, and car repair.

ACTIVITIES:　　4-year member high school morning weight-lifting club
2-year member high school spirit club
1-year member high school business club

INTERESTS:　　Customizing vans
Attending NASCAR races
Racing motorcycles

REFERENCES PROVIDED ON REQUEST

LINDA JEAN COLLINS
5071 Illinois Road
Santa Fe, NM 87504
(505)555-5452

EDUCATION

9/90-present   **College of Santa Fe**, anticipate Bachelor's degree in Theological Studies (with Honors), June 1995. Current GPA: 3.7/4.0

EXPERIENCE

7/94-9/94   **Counselor**, Hill Top Lodge, Albuquerque, NM. Led Bible studies, taught athletics and lifestyle seminars for high schoolers.

10/92-12/93   **Security Agent**, Santa Fe College Bookstore. Handled surveillance activities and arrest of violators. Also, ensured store safety and transported funds.

6/90-9/92   **Services Department**, Osee, Ling (law firm), Santa Fe, NM. Dealt with court filings, courier, mail, and distribution. Acted as receptionist.

1991-present   **Tutor**, Santa Fe College Christian Ministries Tutoring program. Volunteer on a weekly basis with an underprivileged child.

1990-present   **College Fellowship**, Santa Fe Presbyterian Church. Led small group Bible studies, coordinated welcoming and hospitality committees, participated in prayer groups, served at soup kitchens and children's camps.

ADDITIONAL INFORMATION

- Participated with my high school youth group on several work projects at churches and orphanages in Mexico.

- **Treasurer**, Chi Omega House, Santa Fe College.

- **Social Chairman**, Chi Omega Sorority.

References available upon request.

JASMINE K. LAKE

Present Address:
P.O. Box 04834
Baltimore, MD 21218
(301)555-0523

Permanent Address:
5606 Castle Avenue
Langston, OK 73050
(405)555-3247

OBJECTIVE: To obtain a position in the entering class of a top medical school and pursue a career in research-oriented medicine.

EDUCATION: Johns Hopkins University, Baltimore, MD
Bachelor of Science, Biology, with Honors, June 1995
Overall GPA: 3.63   Science GPA: 3.69

RESEARCH EXPERIENCE:

<u>Research Investigator</u>, Molecular Endocrinology Lab, Johns Hopkins Medical Center (1992-1994). Studied the relationship between stem cell factor protein and the Sertoli cell only and germ cell arrest male infertility syndromes. Assisted on projects studying inhibin protein transcription and translation rates. Helped plan, coordinate, and carry out research. Learned and used techniques such as Southern blots, cell cultures, reverse transcriptase polymerase chain reactions, and single-stranded conformational polymorphism. Prepared data and reports for publication.

<u>Research and Clinical Assistant</u>, Department of Neurology, Baltimore Veteran's Administration Outpatient Clinic (1991). Studied neuromuscular diseases and the ability of human muscle to survive different methods of storage. Learned a variety of pathology techniques. Assisted with neurological examinations such as EEGs.

OTHER WORK EXPERIENCE:

<u>Tutor</u>, Johns Hopkins University, Baltimore, MD (1991-1992). Assisted other students with English, mathematics, physics, and biology.

ADDITIONAL INFORMATION:

- <u>Member</u>, Student Radio Board of Directors, Johns Hopkins University.
- <u>Volunteer</u>, "Tiny Tots" Nursery School, Johns Hopkins Special Olympics, Drunk Driving Prevention Program, and Free Peer Tutoring.
- <u>Member</u>, Committee on Housing and Residential Education, Johns Hopkins University.

REFERENCES: Available upon your request.

Stephanie Jane White

Present Address:
P.O. Box 5041
Slidell, LA 70460
(504)555-2398

Permanent Address:
7893 Virginian Lane
Ashland, KY 41101
(606)555-1365

Education:

Grantham College of Engineering - 9/91 to present
Expected to graduate in 6/95 with Bachelor's degree in
Computer Engineering.

Experience:

Summer Intern   6/94 - 9/94
Tandem Computers, Slidell, LA

- Worked with Mechanical Design Group
- Managed the receiving and shipping of prototype parts
- Assembled and evaluated prototype parts and systems
- Re-designed problem parts
- Edited and prepared graphic design for departmental handbook

Part-Time Intern   4/93 - 9/93
Pillar Corporation, Ashland, KY

- Learned the inside workings of a small design consulting firm
- Researched current products to focus design of new concepts
- Designed ideas for new dinnerware sets

Summer Intern   6/92 - 9/92
Praxis Design Inc., Ashland, KY

- Used visual editors to alter program resources
- Edited program code
- Designed program icons and screens

Current Activities:

Member, Kappa Kappa Gamma Sorority

Hobbies:

Skiing, biking, camping, hiking, running, and playing the
violin

Language Skills:

Fluent in German

Chapter Six

SAMPLE COVER LETTERS

732 Strathmore Ave.
Los Angeles, CA 90024

January 4, 19__

Joseph Ream
Hayes & Co.
2400 Wilshire Blvd.
Los Angeles, CA 90024

Dear Mr. Ream:

Sam Johnson of Joseph Brothers referred me to you because of your firm's emphasis on raising venture funds for small to mid-sized businesses. I would be very interested in discussing opportunities in an area that would best utilize my talents.

I will be graduating from UCLA in May 19__. My studies at UCLA have prepared me well to contribute to your organization. My quantitative skills have been sharpened by course work in calculus and statistics.

At Joseph Brothers, I received first-hand exposure to the evaluation of real estate properties for sale or financing. I believe that the tools I acquired there could be effectively translated to analyzing businesses.

My resume is enclosed for your review. I will call you on Friday to set up an appointment to talk about how I might be useful to Hayes & Co. I look forward to meeting with you.

Sincerely,

Amanda Caine

Enclosure.

P.O. Box 5041
Slidell, LA 70460
April 20, 19__

Knute Jameson
Entergy
Employment Department
225 Baronne St.
New Orleans, LA 70112

Dear Mr. Jameson:

This letter is in response to your advertisement in the *New Orleans Picayune* on April 19, 19__ for a design consultant.

Currently, I am pursuing my bachelor's degree in computer engineering at Grantham College of Engineering. I plan to graduate in June 19__. I have taken several courses in computer programming as part of my major and feel confident of my ability to learn and master any design programs.

Through my summer employment, I have gained practical experience in design concepts using computer programming. I believe that my work experience will allow me to make an immediate and valuable contribution to Entergy.

As requested, I am enclosing my resume for your review. I would appreciate the opportunity to discuss my qualifications and abilities in more depth at an interview.

Sincerely Yours,

Stephanie Jane White
(504)555-2398

enclosure

48 Hickory Drive
Houston, TX 77002
(713)555-4968

May 23, 19__

Joseph Lanz
Lanz and Associates at Law
2100 Main Street
Houston, TX 77002

Dear Mr. Lanz:

Thank you for talking with me on May 22, 19__ about the secretarial assistant position available at your office. After speaking with you, I find that I am very interested in becoming a member of your staff. With my past work experience and extensive course work in accounting, mathematics, and typing (55 wpm), I feel that I could be a valuable resource to Lanz and Associates at Law.

This June, I will graduate from Victoria High School. Should I be hired by your law firm, I would be available to work full time from the 12th of June to the 24th of August. From August 24th on, I would be able to work a maximum of five hours each day. My work hours would be reduced because I will be attending college.

Thank you for your time. I look forward to hearing from you soon.

Sincerely,

Heather Moreno

August 20, 19__

Lamplight Restaurant
941 Second Street
Manchester, NH 03036

To Whom It May Concern:

I am writing in response to Lamplight Restaurant's advertisement in the *New Hampshire Sunday News*. The position of part-time cashier greatly interests me.

This fall, I will be a full-time student at Notre Dame College majoring in psychology. I am seeking a position such as yours that will permit me to attend classes while partly financing my education.

The enclosed resume illustrates my experience working as a cashier. I would be pleased if you contacted me for an interview at your earliest convenience. Thank you.

Sincerely,

Elly G. Minch
245 Chaparral Drive
Chester, NH 03036
(603)555-1364

enclosure

July 1, 19__

Ronald Wright
Travel Tours
354 High St.
Springfield, OH 45501

Dear Mr. Wright:

Please accept this letter as my application for the travel agent position available at your firm.

I have just received my diploma from Yellow Springs High School and am excited to begin my career in the travel industry. Presently, I am enrolled in a Regional Occupational Program course and a computer course on the Apollo series. Furthermore, my present employment has enabled me to become an excellent word processor and given me experience in handling correspondence.

I feel that my educational and professional background represent the qualifications you desire for this position. I look forward to setting a date for an interview during which we can discuss the position and share our expectations.

Thank you in advance for your consideration.

Sincerely,

Tracey Warrick
467 Altivo Drive
Yellow Springs, OH 45387
(513)555-1875

Marvin Hopkins
341 Beach Pines Drive
Olympia, WA 98505

July 20, 19__

Annette Tupper
Office of Employment
Computech
11156 Broadway
Redmond, WA 98052

Dear Ms. Tupper:

I have been extremely impressed by your firm's successful entrance into the highly competitive personal computer marketplace. The young and aggressive nature of Computech appeals to me.

As a recent graduate of Eastern Washington University in computer and information sciences, I am looking for a permanent position as a project engineer. Ideally, my employment would entail the possibility for advancement to a management position in research and development.

I worked with Microsoft during my summer vacations in 1992 and 1993. During my employment, I was a member of a four-person team that installed and implemented a 60-node 3Com 3Plus Local Area Network. I have also provided support for both hardware and software of IBM and IBM-compatible personal computers.

A resume is enclosed that reflects my academic, technical, and professional history. I am confident that, with my background, I would be an asset to Computech.

I look forward to hearing from you soon. Thank you for your consideration.

Sincerely,

Marvin Hopkins
(206)555-2397

enclosure

Douglas P. Shaw
191 Cuesta Way
Boise, ID 83706
(208)555-8599

April 6, 19__

Nancy Robbins
The Idaho Statesman
440 Lincoln St.
Boise, ID 83706

Dear Ms. Robbins:

I am writing to you with the hope that there is an opening for a photographer at your newspaper.

For four years, I have been a photographic assistant at Precious Moments Photography. I set up the lights and cameras, mix chemicals, develop film, and print photographs. As head photographer for my high school's yearbook, I took photographs of my classmates at sporting and social activities throughout the year. Some of these photographs were used in your newspaper's sports section.

I am hard-working, creative, and imaginative. I enjoy challenging work and perform well under pressure. I believe that these traits could be useful in highlighting news events for your newspaper.

I would appreciate the opportunity to meet with you to discuss any openings for photographers. I thank you for your consideration and look forward to hearing from you.

Sincerely,

Douglas P. Shaw

MELISSA L. JUNG

1530 HANSEN LANE
DOVER, DE 19901
(302)555-9401

June 12, 19__

Ms. Joanne Tibbots
Dover Unified School District
287 Elementary Ave.
Dover, DE 19901

Dear Ms. Tibbots:

I am writing to inquire whether the Dover Unified School District has an opening for an elementary school teacher. Having a master's degree in education and experience as an assistant teacher, I feel that I am well-qualified to be a teacher.

My personal experience as a mother of four children and as a hostess for six foreign exchange students has taught me how to relate effectively with young people. In addition, I have demonstrated my firm commitment to the community by leading the fund-raising efforts for the new elementary school and serving meals to homeless people at the soup kitchen.

I would appreciate the opportunity to discuss my qualifications and abilities with you at length in an interview.

Sincerely,

Melissa L. Jung

765 Murphy's Lane
Arlington, VA 22207

May 15, 19__

Arlington Motors
Service Department
4900 Speedway
Arlington, VA 22207

Dear Mr. Evans:

I am interested in becoming an automotive mechanic for Arlington Motors. I also would like to participate in the automotive training program that your dealership sponsors.

While attending Arlington High School, I took all the automotive courses offered as well as business math. During the past year, I have been a station attendant at the Arlington Shell. I have made minor repairs to customers' cars and helped the station's mechanics with major repairs. In my free time I customize vans.

I would like to meet with you to discuss opportunities at Arlington Motors. I can be reached by telephone at (703)555-3099. Thank you for your time.

Sincerely,

Roger Newton

BRAIN KANEKO
P.O. Box 4855
Berkeley, CA 94720
(415)555-1007

February 10, 19__

Ms. Judy Andrews
Mesa Engineering
3500 Camelback
Phoenix, AZ 85032

Dear Ms. Andrews:

I am interested in interviewing on campus with a representative of your firm for the entry-level construction management position.

My education and work experiences have prepared me to contribute to Mesa Engineering. I will receive my master's degree in civil engineering from the University of California/Berkeley in May. My course work has focused on construction management. In addition, my summer work experiences have honed my technical and organizational skills on projects.

A copy of my resume is enclosed for your evaluation. If you need further information, I will be pleased to provide you with the necessary materials.

I look forward to meeting with a representative of your firm to discuss my qualifications.

Sincerely,

Brian Kaneko

Enclosure

September 1, 19__

Dr. Melissa Water
PT Clinic
5550 First Avenue
Grand Rapids, MI 49505

Dear Dr. Water:

I am writing concerning possible employment opportunities with your clinic. In particular, I am looking for an assistant physical therapist position that would permit me to work with physically disabled individuals while I attend college.

In September, I will start Calvin College where I plan to major in education of the physically handicapped. I would be available for part-time work at that time.

I have had direct experience in dealing with physically disabled people. At Bay de Noc Camp, I was camp counselor for developmentally disabled teenagers and adults and at Escanaba High School I assisted the Special Education teacher.

I would be delighted to meet with you at your convenience to discuss opportunities at your clinic.

Sincerely,

Christianna M. Nelson
900 Bear Valley Drive
Escanaba, MI 49829
(906)555-2380

Dale Crivello

257 Huntington Drive
Middlebury, VT 05753

August 20, 19__

Manager
Covington Inn
300 Main Street
Montpelier, VT 05602

Dear Manager:

I am writing in response to your advertisement in the August 19, 19__ issue of the *Times Argus*. I would appreciate the opportunity to talk to you about your inn's need for a preparation cook.

In Middlebury, I was the preparation cook for Denny's Restaurant. I was responsible for making all salads including Chef's, Caesar, and Shrimp Louis. This fall I will be attending the New England Culinary Institute where I plan to major in food production, management, and services. I am confident that my past experience and present training would be of benefit to your inn's restaurant.

Thank you for your consideration. I hope to have a chance to speak with you about the position.

Sincerely,

Dale Crivello
(802)555-4294

ELIZABETH M. LEIGH-WOOD

387 SUNNY HILLS DRIVE
MADISON, WI 53711
(608)555-1524

May 14, 19__

Ms. Janet Smith
Madison Community Recreation Center
1500 Second Ave.
Madison, WI 53711

Dear Ms. Smith:

I am writing to follow up on our May 13th telephone conversation about the lifeguard position. As we discussed, I have been certified in Standard First Aid and CPR. In August, I will attend the University of Wisconsin on a swimming scholarship. Furthermore, I was a lifeguard for Sunny Hills Neighborhood Club Pool during the summer of 1992.

If I meet your requirements, I would be available for employment from June 1st to August 15th.

My resume is enclosed as you requested. I look forward to hearing from you soon.

Sincerely,

Elizabeth M. Leigh-Wood

enclosure

217 Arthur Avenue
Omaha, NE 69337
(308)555-5003

September 10, 19__

Bob Perkins
Superintendent
Sunburst Golf Course
One Sunburst Way
Phoenix, AZ 85021

Dear Mr. Perkins:

I wish to apply for a position as greenskeeper. John Niles of Oak Brook Golf Course told me about this opening and suggested that I contact you.

Currently, I am the supervisor at Sugar Hill Nursery in Omaha. I have become familiar with the care of many varieties of grasses, trees, plants, and shrubs. Also, I took horticulture and biology courses in high school. I am self-motivated and work well independently.

I will call you next week to follow up this letter. Thank you in advance for your consideration.

Sincerely,

John Nowark

CRAIG L. HJORRING

31 Anderson Road ● Fort Collins, CO 80523 ● (303)555-0469

February 10, 19__

Mr. Richard Carmichael
Sports Plus
11135 Silverado Trail
Denver, CO 80202

Dear Mr. Carmichael:

I would be very interested in talking with you about a marketing career at Sports Plus.

Presently, I am pursuing my bachelor's degree in business administration and management with an emphasis in marketing. I plan to graduate in May 19__.

During the past three summers, I have worked at Sutherland Sports Wear. I started as a sales representative and was promoted to assistant regional sales manager. The following are a few of my accomplishments that may interest your organization:

- Decreased advertising costs by 2.8% of sales.
- Increased sales by 14% during a 3-month period.
- Made industry contacts for joint venture opportunities.

I feel that my qualifications would enable me to be a productive member of your marketing team.

Enclosed is my resume for your review. I look forward to meeting with you to discuss employment opportunities at Sports Plus.

Sincerely,

Craig L. Hjorring

Enclosure

3089 Mc Glenn Drive
Jonesboro, AR 72467
(501)555-9268
January 4, 19__

Dr. Sally Clark
Sally's Veterinary Hospital
3452 Creekside Lane
Little Rock, AR 72202

Dear Dr. Clark:

I am interested in applying for employment as a veterinarian assistant.

Recently, I graduated from Arkansas State University with a degree in veterinary science. Also, I have 6 months of experience working as a veterinarian assistant. My duties included feeding and bathing the animals, administering medication, and assisting in treatment of the animals. I believe that my education and work experience would enable me to be a valuable asset to your hospital.

I would like to meet with you and demonstrate that I have the qualifications and the personality that make for a successful veterinarian assistant. I can be contacted at the above telephone number. Many thanks for your consideration.

Sincerely,

Nicole Anne Chang

Josephine Elizabeth Crocker

March 23, 19__

Ms. Deborah Black
Human Resources
New Jersey Health Department
P.O. Box 3000
Trenton, NJ 08625

Dear Ms. Black:

This letter is in response to your advertisement for an environmental health inspector that appeared in *The Trentonian* on March 22, 19__ . Please accept my resume in consideration for this position.

With a degree from Trenton State College in environmental health science and two internships with county health departments in the environmental division, I believe that I am well-suited to the state's health department needs.

Thank you for your time. I look forward to hearing from you soon regarding the position.

Sincerely,

Josephine E. Crocker
P.O. Box 317 A
Trenton, NJ 08625
(609)555-4832

502 Sleigh Street
Stockton, CA 95211

January 20, 19__

Mr. Oliver Ford
International Bank
500 Park Ave.
New York, NY 10010

Dear Mr. Ford:

I am writing to obtain further information regarding employment with your organization as a financial analyst. I strongly believe that international banking is an area in which my academic training and personal qualities would be an asset.

At the University of the Pacific, I am majoring in political science while also pursuing a business focus. Course work in accounting, statistics, and management has allowed me to develop the skills that will be necessary to successfully perform financial analyses. Moreover, my past work experiences have provided me opportunities to use and refine those skills in a business setting.

I appreciate your time and consideration. I hope to have the opportunity to talk with you in the near future.

Sincerely,

George Cox

Nolan T. Yu

P.O. Box 61434, Cambridge, MA 02139   (617)555-6087

March 15, 19__

Ms. Jessica Peters
Dynamic Consulting Group
250 Michigan Ave.
Chicago, IL 60680

Dear Ms. Peters:

I would greatly appreciate the opportunity to talk to you about your firm's need for a consultant. I believe that my education at the Massachusetts Institute of Technology in computer and information sciences as well as my technical expertise would be useful to your computer consulting group.

Working at Dynamic Consulting Group would be a unique and challenging experience. Your company has attracted me by virtue of its size and reputation in the field of consulting.

I appreciate your time and consideration. I look forward to hearing from you soon.

Sincerely,

Nolan T. Yu

VGM CAREER BOOKS

CAREER DIRECTORIES
Careers Encyclopedia
Dictionary of Occupational Titles
Occupational Outlook Handbook

CAREERS FOR
Animal Lovers
Bookworms
Caring People
Computer Buffs
Crafty People
Culture Lovers
Environmental Types
Film Buffs
Foreign Language Aficionados
Good Samaritans
Gourmets
History Buffs
Kids at Heart
Nature Lovers
Night Owls
Number Crunchers
Plant Lovers
Shutterbugs
Sports Nuts
Travel Buffs
Writers

CAREERS IN
Accounting; Advertising;
Business; Child Care;
Communications; Computers;
Education; Engineering;
the Environment; Finance;
Government; Health Care; High
Tech; International Business;
Journalism; Law; Marketing;
Medicine; Science; Social &
Rehabilitation Services

CAREER PLANNING
Admissions Guide to Selective
   Business Schools
Beating Job Burnout
Beginning Entrepreneur
Career Planning & Development
   for College Students & Recent
   Graduates
Career Change
Careers Checklists
Complete Guide to Career
   Etiquette
Cover Letters They Don't Forget
Dr. Job's Complete Career Guide

Executive Job Search Strategies
Guide to Basic Cover Letter
   Writing
Guide to Basic Résumé Writing
Guide to Temporary
   Employment
Job Interviewing for College
   Students
Joyce Lain Kennedy's Career
   Book
Out of Uniform
Slam Dunk Résumés

CAREER PORTRAITS
Animals; Cars; Computers;
Electronics; Fashion;
Firefighting; Music; Nursing;
Sports; Teaching; Travel; Writing

GREAT JOBS FOR
Communications Majors
Engineering Majors
English Majors
Foreign Language Majors
History Majors
Psychology Majors

HOW TO
Approach an Advertising Agency
   and Walk Away with the Job
   You Want
Bounce Back Quickly After
   Losing Your Job
Choose the Right Career
Cómo escribir un currículum
   vitae en inglés que tenga éxito
Find Your New Career Upon
   Retirement
Get & Keep Your First Job
Get Hired Today
Get into the Right Business
   School
Get into the Right Law School
Get People to Do Things Your
   Way
Have a Winning Job Interview
Hit the Ground Running in Your
   New Job
Hold It All Together When
   You've Lost Your Job
Improve Your Study Skills
Jump Start a Stalled Career
Land a Better Job

Launch Your Career in TV News
Make the Right Career Moves
Market Your College Degree
Move from College into a
   Secure Job
Negotiate the Raise You Deserve
Prepare a Curriculum Vitae
Prepare for College
Run Your Own Home Business
Succeed in College
Succeed in High School
Take Charge of Your Child's
   Early Education
Write a Winning Résumé
Write Successful Cover Letters
Write Term Papers & Reports
Write Your College Application
   Essay

MADE EASY
Cover Letters
Job Hunting
Job Interviews
Résumés

OPPORTUNITIES IN
This extensive series provides
detailed information on nearly
150 individual career fields.

RÉSUMÉS FOR
Advertising Careers
Banking and Financial Careers
Business Management Careers
College Students &
   Recent Graduates
Communications Careers
Education Careers
Engineering Careers
Environmental Careers
Ex-Military Personnel
50+ Job Hunters
Health and Medical Careers
High School Graduates
High Tech Careers
Law Careers
Midcareer Job Changes
Re-Entering the Job Market
Sales and Marketing Careers
Scientific and Technical Careers
Social Service Careers
The First-Time Job Hunter

 VGM Career Horizons
a division of *NTC Publishing Group*
4255 West Touhy Avenue
Lincolnwood, Illinois 60646–1975